Strategic Disruption by Special Operations Forces

A Concept for Proactive Campaigning Short of Traditional War

ERIC ROBINSON, TIMOTHY R. HEATH, GABRIELLE TARINI, DANIEL EGEL, MACE MOESNER IV, CHRISTIAN CURRIDEN, DEREK GROSSMAN, SALE LILLY

Prepared for the United States Army
Approved for public release; distribution unlimited

For more information on this publication, visit **www.rand.org/t/RRA1794-1**.

About RAND

The RAND Corporation is a research organization that develops solutions to public policy challenges to help make communities throughout the world safer and more secure, healthier and more prosperous. RAND is nonprofit, nonpartisan, and committed to the public interest. To learn more about RAND, visit www.rand.org.

Research Integrity

Our mission to help improve policy and decisionmaking through research and analysis is enabled through our core values of quality and objectivity and our unwavering commitment to the highest level of integrity and ethical behavior. To help ensure our research and analysis are rigorous, objective, and nonpartisan, we subject our research publications to a robust and exacting quality-assurance process; avoid both the appearance and reality of financial and other conflicts of interest through staff training, project screening, and a policy of mandatory disclosure; and pursue transparency in our research engagements through our commitment to the open publication of our research findings and recommendations, disclosure of the source of funding of published research, and policies to ensure intellectual independence. For more information, visit www.rand.org/about/research-integrity.

RAND's publications do not necessarily reflect the opinions of its research clients and sponsors.

About This Report

This report documents research and analysis conducted as part of a project entitled *Army Special Operations Roles and Priorities in Competition with China*, sponsored by United States Army Special Operations Command (USASOC). The purpose of the project was to identify and prioritize potential contributions of Army special operations forces to efforts to impose costs, create dilemmas, and affect adversarial decisionmaking to advance U.S. influence and erode adversary influence during competition and in key contingencies involving China.

This research was conducted within RAND Arroyo Center's Strategy, Doctrine, and Resources Program. RAND Arroyo Center, part of the RAND Corporation, is a federally funded research and development center (FFRDC) sponsored by the United States Army.

RAND operates under a "Federal-Wide Assurance" (FWA00003425) and complies with the *Code of Federal Regulations for the Protection of Human Subjects Under United States Law* (45 CFR 46), also known as "the Common Rule," as well as with the implementation guidance set forth in DoD Instruction 3216.02. As applicable, this compliance includes reviews and approvals by RAND's Institutional Review Board (the Human Subjects Protection Committee) and by the U.S. Army. The views of sources utilized in this report are solely their own and do not represent the official policy or position of DoD or the U.S. government.

Acknowledgments

We are indebted to the many representatives of the U.S. special operations community who supported this effort, and we are particularly thankful for insights from the soldiers and civilians at USASOC Headquarters, 1st Special Forces Command, 4th Psychological Operations Group, 8th Psychological Operations Group, 95th Civil Affairs Brigade, U.S. Special Operations Command Pacific, and the Office of the Assistant Secretary of Defense for Special Operations and Low-Intensity Conflict. We are especially thankful for support from our sponsors within USASOC Headquarters, including COL Joseph Wortham, Matthew Carran, Larry Deel, Brooke Tannehill, and Damon Cussen.

This research benefited tremendously from detailed peer reviews by Adam Grissom of RAND and Seth G. Jones of the Center for Strategic and International Studies. We are also thankful to LTG (ret.) Charles T. Cleveland for his insights and feedback throughout this research. Similarly, we thank the leadership of the RAND Arroyo Center for its support throughout this project, including Sally Sleeper, Molly Dunigan, Jonathan Wong, Stephen Watts, and Jennifer Kavanagh (now of the Carnegie Endowment for International Peace). All errors or omissions remain the sole responsibility of the authors.

Summary

Multiple iterations of national strategic guidance in recent years have directed the U.S. military to embrace strategic competition as a primary defense priority. The central theme of this guidance has been the need to deter aggression and prepare to fight a major war with a strategic competitor should deterrence fail.

Yet little consensus exists as to how the U.S. military should address another critical aspect of strategic competition—specifically, attempts by these same competitors to achieve their own objectives without fighting, through means short of war. More broadly, there is recognition that U.S. competitors employ a range of tools beyond the threat of conventional military aggression to challenge U.S. interests. While much has been written about the military's role in responding to such challenges, there is little agreement as to the military's role in proactively disrupting these approaches short of war. More specifically, the mechanisms through which such disruptive approaches can enable strategic gains—including through efforts to impose costs, create dilemmas, and target adversary vulnerabilities—are even less well understood.

This research seeks to answer two core questions to inform this debate. First, what are the mechanisms through which disruption campaigns by military forces can enable friendly strategic outcomes short of war? Second, what is the role for special operations forces (SOF) in such campaigns?

To answer these questions, this report develops and presents a new concept for *strategic disruption*. Drawing from interviews with dozens of defense policymakers and planners as our foundation, we gathered and analyzed an expansive set of 50 historical case studies of disruption campaigns by SOF and similar units that enabled or pursued strategic objectives. Across these historical cases, we explored how strategic disruption campaigns can set favorable conditions to achieve national objectives through deliberate efforts to delay, degrade, or deny an adversary's ability to achieve core interests via their own preferred courses of action. The goal of this research was not to assess the efficacy of each campaign. Our aim was more foundational—to lay a conceptual basis for how SOF can leverage such disruption in the pursuit of friendly strategic objectives across multiple instruments of national power.

We found that the value proposition of SOF in this form of campaigning is to frustrate adversary-preferred strategies through five unique pillars of capability—*resist, support, influence, understand,* and *target*—to create the time, space, and opportunities needed for the United States to achieve strategic objectives across multiple elements of national power. More specifically, our analysis revealed a series of mechanisms through which SOF-led strategic disruption has historically sought to deny adversary objectives in the pursuit of friendly diplomatic, informational, military, and economic aims.

The Logic of Strategic Disruption

In our concept for strategic disruption, friendly forces conduct individual tactical actions, or a series of tactical actions as part of an operational-level campaign, that are designed to frustrate some aspect of an adversary's preferred strategy to achieve their core national interests. These disruptive campaigns do not need to produce strategic effects in and of themselves. Rather, they are designed to delay, degrade, or deny an adversary's ability to achieve any number of broader diplomatic, informational, military, or economic (DIME) interests. Specifically, these disruptive campaigns are meant to impose costs or create dilemmas that limit an adversary's ability to achieve their core interests through preferred courses of action. This often involves efforts by the friendly actor to target underlying vulnerabilities in the adversary's preferred approach. Implicit in this concept is that the adversary's preferred course of action is the one assessed as most likely to achieve strategic objectives.

To use an analogy, strategic disruption is more than just responding to an opponent's last move on the chess board. Instead, it is deliberately moving pieces across the board to constrain an opponent's options for their next move and frustrating their preferred strategy for victory. Ultimately, these disruptive effects create the time, space and opportunities for the friendly government to leverage multiple tools of national power—not just military ones—to achieve its own strategic objectives. The logic of this approach is summarized in Figure S.1.

An example, drawn from the historical analysis presented in this report, helps to explain this logic. From 1956–1971, the U.S. Central Intelligence Agency (CIA) conducted a deliberate paramilitary campaign (with support from the Department of Defense) to support Tibetan resistance fighters against Chinese Communist Party (CCP) occupation and rule.[1] These efforts degraded the ability of the CCP to assert the legitimacy of its rule over Tibet (a core strategic priority) by forcing it to devote additional resources to consolidating local control (contrary to the preferred approach). Ultimately, this campaign helped generate strategic diplomatic advantage for the United States by providing bargaining advantages during the Nixon administration's efforts to pursue a Sino-U.S. rapprochement in the early 1970s, exploiting the broader souring of Sino-Soviet relations at the time.

This classic example of unconventional warfare represents just one approach to strategic disruption explored throughout this report. More generally, it highlights three foundational tenets of our concept that apply across other historical examples of SOF and SOF-like forces attempting similar strategic disruption of adversary core interests:

- **Strategic disruption is proactive:** Strategic disruption provides a mechanism for military forces to gain deliberate advantage in campaigning short of war and set the conditions in which competition occurs, rather than simply react to adversary coercion.

---

[1] U.S. Department of State, "33.7 Memorandum for the Special Group," in *Foreign Relations of the United States, 1964-1968*: Vol. XXX, *China*, January 9, 1964. For more background, see Mikel Dunham, *Buddha's Warriors: The Story of the CIA-Backed Tibetan Freedom Fighters, the Chinese Communist Invasion, and the Ultimate Fall of Tibet*, Penguin, 2004.

FIGURE S.1
The Logic of Strategic Disruption

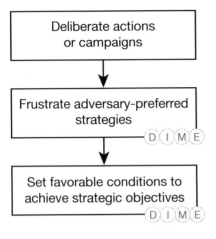

A friendly actor conducts deliberate actions or campaigns intended to frustrate an adversary's strategic or operational design.

These activities delay, degrade, or deny an adversary's ability to achieve core DIME interests (across the DIME spectrum) through their preferred courses of action, often by targeting vulnerabilities in the adversary's preferred approach.

These disruptive effects create time, space, and opportunities to achieve friendly strategic DIME objectives.

- **Strategic disruption seeks to frustrate adversary-preferred strategies:** Strategic disruption enables military forces during campaigning to interrupt an adversary's strategic or operational design by complicating the adversary's ability to achieve their own strategic objectives through preferred courses of action.
- **Strategic disruption enables multiple instruments of national power:** Strategic disruption sets favorable conditions for multiple instruments of national power to achieve strategic objectives across the DIME spectrum.

SOF's Role in Strategic Disruption

This report focuses specifically on the role for SOF to contribute to strategic disruption during campaigning. We begin by exploring various theories of SOF's strategic potential in wartime and competition. We then explore SOF's specific value proposition in our concept for strategic disruption. SOF's strategic potential lies not in their unilateral military strength, which is limited relative to conventional military forces. Instead, we assess that SOF's value proposition in strategic disruption is their ability to frustrate adversary-preferred strategies through five unique pillars of capabilities—resist, support, influence, understand, and target—to create time, space, and opportunities to achieve strategic objectives across major elements of national power.

These pillars represent a framework through which we can better understand SOF's ability to conduct strategic disruption that generates favorable conditions (that is, creating time, space, and opportunities) for multiple elements of national power to achieve broader strategic objectives. They are summarized below:

1. The **resist pillar** involves efforts to enable a resistance or insurgency to coerce, disrupt, or overthrow a government or occupying power or deter an occupation.
2. The **support pillar** involves efforts to build the capacity of foreign security forces and enable their own efforts to defend against internal or external threats to their security.
3. The **influence pillar** involves efforts to inform and shape the attitudes, behavior, and decisions of foreign actors in support of U.S. interests.
4. The **understand pillar** involves efforts to extract strategically relevant information from politically sensitive, contested, or denied environments.
5. The **target pillar** involves efforts to seize, destroy, disrupt, or secure key personnel, equipment, or infrastructure in politically sensitive, contested, or denied environments.

We explored SOF's value proposition for strategic disruption across each of these pillars using a variety of primary and secondary data sources. Our underlying concept for strategic disruption, and SOF's role in it, was informed by 37 detailed interviews with defense policymakers and military personnel at the tactical, operational, and strategic levels that helped frame this concept, as well as a comprehensive review of the growing literature on the role for military forces in strategic competition short of war, prior research and analysis on the role for SOF in strategic competition, and associated military doctrine. The bulk of the analysis presented in this report was then premised on an expansive and detailed review of 50 publicly documented historical cases of strategic disruption, drawn from hundreds of public accounts of historical efforts by SOF and SOF-like forces to frustrate adversary-preferred strategies. Although our intent was to produce as comprehensive a set of prior cases of strategic disruption as is publicly available, there are certainly examples we missed. Instead, the aim of this approach was to provide a stronger conceptual basis, rooted in historical experience, for the strategic potential of military forces to disrupt adversary efforts to achieve objectives through means other than war.

We leveraged these historical cases to derive a comprehensive series of mechanisms through which SOF and similar forces can leverage our five pillars of capabilities for strategic disruption—resist, support, influence, understand, and target—to frustrate adversary-preferred strategies and enable strategic outcomes across the DIME spectrum throughout history. These mechanisms are summarized below in Table S.1.

Findings and Implications

This historical analysis generated several findings related to the strategic potential of this approach for SOF, summarized in Table S.2 and organized across each of the three core tenets of strategic disruption.

This research has broad applicability to military and even nonmilitary policymakers, planners, and actors seeking a conceptual framework and logic for enabling strategic effects in competition short of war. Along these lines, a separate, companion report applies this framework for strategic disruption to a detailed playbook of potential Chinese People's Liberation Army missions, tasks, and vulnerabilities in both peacetime competition and in the event of a simmering, low-intensity conflict between China and the United States.

More importantly, this research provides concrete examples and a clear rationale for the unique potential of SOF to frustrate adversary competitive strategies, particularly in situations in which conventional deterrence alone is an insufficient tool to achieve similar effects. Absent such a capability, the U.S. military is left to choose between ill-suited escalatory responses as its only recourse to adversary approaches that deliberately seek to avoid high-end conflict.

TABLE S.1

Mechanisms for SOF's Strategic Disruption Across the DIME Spectrum

SOF Capability	Diplomatic Competition	Informational Competition	Military Competition	Economic Competition
Resist	• Incentivize a change in adversary policy • Shape resistance movements	• Undermine adversary legitimacy	• Fix adversary conventional forces • Deter adversary aggression through resistance	• Extend an adversary to commit resources • Disrupt or sabotage critical infrastructure
Support	• Incentivize diplomatic settlements • Shape partner's policy preferences	• Expand influence in contested areas • Deny adversary objectives through resilience	• Promote benefits of military-to-military relations • Deny adversary objectives through internal stability	• Buy time for long-term economic assistance
Influence	• Undermine adversary legitimacy • Enhance support for diplomacy	• Disrupt adversary narratives through strategic messaging	• Deceive adversary understanding of friendly strength • Undermine adversary morale	• Buy time for long-term economic assistance
Understand	• Expand diplomatic engagement with local populations • Share strategic intelligence with partners	• Inform population-centric messaging campaigns	• Support operations in population-centric campaigns • Enable conventional operations • Enable targeting	• Inform economic/humanitarian assistance • Identify economic vulnerabilities to sabotage
Target	• Incentivize diplomatic settlements • Control escalation through limited use of force	• Generate adversary uncertainty over operational reach • Degrade adversary morale and will	• Target critical infrastructure • Generate iterative, network disruption	• Degrade adversary resources base through sabotage

TABLE S.2

Key Findings Related to the Core Tenets of Strategic Disruption

Core Tenets	Key Findings
Strategic Disruption is Proactive	• Proactive attempts at strategic disruption can enable *direct and immediate* strategic outcomes, often in a time-bound manner, to clear a specific hurdle to the success of some friendly strategic objective. • Proactive attempts at strategic disruption can also enable *indirect and delayed* strategic outcomes, shaping broader conditions in which strategic competition and potential conflict is likely to occur over longer-durations to enable strategic success.
Strategic Disruption Frustrates Adversary-preferred Strategies	• Efforts to frustrate adversary-preferred strategies often enable strategic success by incentivizing an adversary to embrace suboptimal approaches. • Efforts to frustrate adversary-preferred strategies, rather than simply deter by punishment or direct cost imposition, can help manage escalation. • Efforts to frustrate adversary-preferred strategies do not need to be strategic in and of themselves to enable strategic disruption.
Strategic Disruption Enables Multiple Instruments of National Power	• Disruptive effects on adversary-preferred strategies in one domain can often create the time, space, and opportunities for strategic success in another domain. • Not all strategic opportunities created by strategic disruption campaigns across the DIME spectrum were known in advance of the initial deliberate employment of forces, and such opportunities often materialized in the course of executing disruption campaigns.

Specifically, this research provides a clear rubric for SOF-focused policymakers and leadership to motivate future concepts, plans, and analysis examining ways to harness SOF's unique potential to execute disruptive campaigns that challenge nation-state competitors' efforts to win without fighting. In our work, we found the following:

- Success in strategic disruption should be measured by whether such campaigns are initially able to frustrate an adversary's preferred strategy.
- Strategic disruption requires deep understanding of adversary strategies and priorities. Leaders should invest in efforts to probe and understand an adversary's preferred courses of action, risk tolerance, and escalation thresholds as a foundational task.
- Strategic disruption requires flexible yet specific campaign plans and headquarters with a long-term focus to manage campaigns over long durations.
- Strategic disruption requires SOF to build interagency partnerships up from the tactical to the national-strategic level.

Contents

Figures and Tables

Figures

Tables

CHAPTER 1

Introducing Strategic Disruption

Multiple iterations of national strategic guidance in recent years have directed the U.S. military to embrace strategic competition as a primary defense priority. The central theme of this guidance has been the need to deter aggression and prepare to fight a major war with a strategic competitor should deterrence fail.

Yet little consensus exists as to how the U.S. military should address another critical aspect of strategic competition—specifically, attempts by these same competitors to achieve their own objectives without fighting, through means short of war with the United States. An abundance of terms has emerged to describe the most potent of such threats, including *hybrid warfare, gray-zone aggression, political warfare,* and countless others. More broadly, there is recognition that the U.S.'s competitors employ a range of tools (beyond the threat of outright military aggression) to challenge U.S. interests and achieve their own strategic goals.

Although much has been written about the military's role in responding to such challenges, there is little agreement as to the military's proper role in proactively disrupting an adversary's ability to leverage such approaches to achieve their own objectives short of an outright conflict. Phrased differently, the mechanisms through which military forces can impose costs, create dilemmas, and target adversary vulnerabilities during competition to deny an adversary a position of competitive advantage are not well understood. Absent such an understanding, the usefulness of these disruptive approaches as a potential competitive strategy is hard to grasp, particularly given their escalatory nature.

This report therefore seeks to answer two core questions to inform this debate. First, what are the mechanisms through which disruption campaigns by military forces can enable friendly strategic outcomes short of war? Second, what is the role for special operations forces (SOF) in such campaigns?

To this end, we explored 50 historical examples of strategic disruption campaigns by SOF and similar units, supported by interviews with dozens of defense policymakers and planners. The concept that emerged throughout our research, which we call *strategic disruption,* can be defined as setting favorable conditions to achieve national objectives through deliberate efforts to delay, degrade, or deny an adversary's ability to achieve core interests via their own preferred courses of action. From this underlying logic, we identified and explored several different mechanisms for how military forces—and SOF specifically—can leverage strategic disruption campaigns in the pursuit of friendly strategic objectives short of war.

Methodology

The research presented in this report is built upon a combination of primary and secondary data sources. The framing for the strategic disruption concept emerged from 37 detailed interviews with defense policymakers and military personnel at the tactical, operational, and strategic levels. These interviewees reflected an opportunistic sample of individuals with special operations–specific expertise, at theater special operations commands, service component commands and headquarters, or the policy level. Interviews focused primarily on exploring different perspectives on the potential for SOF to impose costs, create dilemmas, and target adversary vulnerabilities in strategic competition and on the concepts, capabilities, and structures required to execute such missions. The framing that emerged from these interviews was supplemented by a comprehensive review of the growing literature on the role of military forces in strategic competition short of war, prior research and analysis on the role of SOF in strategic competition, and associated military doctrine.

From these interviews, the research team then analyzed hundreds of public accounts of historical efforts by nation states and other actors to (1) use SOF or SOF-like forces to (2) execute campaigns that disrupt an adversary's preferred strategy—whether by imposing costs, creating dilemmas, or otherwise targeting vulnerabilities in that strategy—that (3) pursued or enabled friendly strategic objectives as a result. Using these three criteria, our systematic review produced an expansive set of 50 publicly documented historical cases of strategic disruption campaigns for analysis throughout this report and summarized in Appendix A. Though our intent was to produce as comprehensive a set of prior cases as is publicly available, there are certainly examples we missed. This includes cases that are not in the public domain, lack a written historical record, or are simply not known to us despite our best efforts to document all cases.

Overall, these historical cases were then used to inductively derive the mechanisms through which SOF and similar forces can frustrate adversary-preferred strategies and enable strategic outcomes across the diplomatic, informational, military, or economic (DIME) spectrum. To that end, our primary goal was to be exhaustive of these various mechanisms for strategic disruption's ensuing strategic-level impact. In so doing, our aim with this research is to create a stronger conceptual basis than exists at present, rooted in historical experience, for the strategic potential of military forces to disrupt adversary efforts to achieve their objectives through means other than war.

Several other aspects of this research design should be highlighted up front to inform interpretation of our analysis in the ensuing chapters. First, it should be made clear that our goal was not to assess the determinants of success of individual strategic disruption campaigns. Some were certainly successful; others were outright failures; most were somewhere in between. A detailed diagnosis of the exact attributes defining successful strategic disruption campaigns is the purview of future research. Instead, our aim was more foundational—to explore the underlying logic of such campaigns and lay a conceptual basis for how SOF can seek to deny an adversary's strategic aims short of war and pursue friendly strategic outcomes along the way.

Second, while our concept is focused primarily on strategic disruption campaigns conducted outside a high-end conventional war, we did include cases of SOF-led strategic disruption campaigns that occurred as discrete components of high-end conflicts. This is primarily because of the potential for SOF-led strategic disruption to occur as part of an indirect, low-intensity conflict between great powers and their proxies—a conflict that might include limited forms of violence in peripheral theaters of competition. Such indirect campaigns certainly came to define the U.S. and Soviet experience during the Cold War and are well represented throughout our case study analysis.

Third, our review of historical cases did not just focus on examples of strategic disruption conducted by U.S. forces alone; we also aimed to capture the experiences of U.S. allies, partners, and even competitors and adversaries.[1] This does not imply any endorsement of the intent of specific adversary operations, nor that the United States should seek to replicate specific tactics employed by these adversaries for its own purposes. Rather, our approach aimed to draw out relevant lessons about how such disruptive activities were used to set conditions for the achievement of strategic outcomes.

Finally, while our focus was on understanding the role for SOF in strategic disruption, we also included historical examples where other types of forces with similar authorities or mandates to operate in politically sensitive or denied environments pursued strategic disruption. We referred to these forces as *SOF-like* throughout this research, incorporating several examples where intelligence and cyber operations forces, as examples, have pursued strategic disruption. This approach was biased toward inclusivity to maximize our understanding of SOF's future strategic potential—whether through alternative applications of current capabilities, or development of new capabilities currently resident in other specialized military or intelligence units. Beyond our historical case analysis, we offer an additional chapter in this report focused on how one set of such capabilities—for cyber and electromagnetic spectrum operations—is likely to affect the tactical ability of SOF to execute disruptive campaigns in the first place.

Structure of This Report

The remainder of this report begins by motivating and describing our underlying concept of strategic disruption as a proactive approach to campaigning short of war. We then explore SOF's role in strategic disruption across five key pillars of SOF capabilities that emerge from an analysis of existing military doctrine for disruption, prior research on the strategic poten-

---

[1] There are likely to be instances of SOF-led strategic disruption by foreign actors that are not adequately documented in English language–based historical records, a clear area for future research to expand this analysis.

tial of SOF, and our own historical analysis. These five pillars—resist, support, influence, understand, and target—are analyzed in the following chapters, which describe historical examples in which SOF or SOF-like forces have delivered strategic effects across DIME objectives. An additional chapter focuses on the potential for emerging technologies to affect SOF's long-term prospects for executing strategic disruption campaigns, with particular emphasis on cyber and electronic warfare capabilities. The report concludes with a chapter summarizing key takeaways for defense policymakers and planners to use in guiding efforts by SOF to enable strategic disruption.

CHAPTER 2

Defining Strategic Disruption

This chapter introduces our concept of strategic disruption—a new concept for campaigning by military forces to actively pursue strategic advantage short of war. *Strategic disruption*, as defined in this report, sets favorable conditions to achieve national objectives through deliberate efforts to delay, degrade, or deny an adversary's ability to achieve core interests via their own preferred courses of action.

This chapter begins by articulating the need for such a concept and proceeds to define three foundational tenets of strategic disruption, summarized as follows:

- **Strategic disruption is proactive:** Strategic disruption provides a mechanism for military forces to gain deliberate advantage in campaigning short of war and set the conditions in which competition occurs, rather than simply react to adversary coercion.
- **Strategic disruption seeks to frustrate adversary-preferred strategies:** Strategic disruption enables military forces during campaigning to interrupt an adversary's strategic or operational design by complicating the ability to achieve their own strategic objectives through preferred courses of action.
- **Strategic disruption enables multiple instruments of national power:** Strategic disruption sets favorable conditions for major instruments of national power to achieve strategic objectives across the DIME spectrum.

Why Strategic Disruption?

Our concept for strategic disruption seeks to inform ongoing debate about the military's role in campaigning short of war, specifically regarding the potential for military forces to deliver strategic effects in support of national objectives during competition. Much has been written about the role of the military instrument of national power short of war, dating back to the 2018 National Defense Strategy (NDS)'s directive for the U.S. military to "expand the competitive space, seizing the initiative to challenge our competitors where we possess advantages and they lack strength."[1] The 2022 NDS carried forward this assessment in slightly different

---

[1] U.S. Department of Defense (DoD), *Summary of the 2018 National Defense Strategy,* January 2018b.

terms, citing the need to "sustain and strengthen deterrence with the People's Republic of China (PRC) as our most consequential strategic competitor."[2]

While both strategies emphasize the role for the military instrument of national power short of war, their guidance highlights a fundamental tension in current thinking on the military's role in achieving national objectives outside an actual war that is yet to be resolved. Since 2018, a steady drumbeat of policymakers and scholars alike have argued that the military's singular role in strategic competition should be to deter conventional aggression and, where that fails, to fight and win the nation's wars.[3] This approach contends that the military's true role short of war is to prepare for it, and that most efforts to secure U.S. national objectives outside declared conflict should be the responsibility of other instruments of national power.[4]

However, a competing argument suggests that a singular focus on deterring conventional aggression is insufficient as a defense strategy, and that the U.S. military must prioritize working in concert with other instruments of national power to actively secure national interests in contested domains. This argument contends that the United States' conventional warfighting strength has actually incentivized adversaries to adopt a competitive strategy that seeks to win without fighting,[5] thereby transforming the United States' often singular focus on preparing for war into a competitive disadvantage.[6]

Ultimately, the 2022 NDS declared that the U.S. military must both prepare for war and compete short of war—leveraging integrated deterrence to prepare for conflict and shape adversary willingness to go to war while actively campaigning for advantage in peacetime. Defining its concept for campaigning, the NDS factsheet declares,

> The United States will operate forces, synchronize broader Department efforts, and align Department activities with other instruments of national power to undermine acute forms of competitor coercion, complicate competitors' military preparations, and develop our own warfighting capabilities together with Allies and partners.[7]

---

[2] DoD, *Fact Sheet: 2022 National Defense Strategy*, fact sheet, March 2022.

[3] See, for example, Jim Mitre and Andre Gellerman, "Defining DoD's Role in Gray Zone Competition," Center for a New American Security, August 24, 2020.

[4] See, for example, Raphael S. Cohen, "It's Time to Drop 'Competition' in the National Defense Strategy," *The Hill*, May 18, 2021.

[5] See, for example, Timothy R. Heath, Derek Grossman, and Asha Clark, *China's Quest for Global Primacy*, RAND Corporation, RR-A447-1, 2021; Alice Hunt Friend and Shannon Culbertson, "Special Obfuscations: The Strategic Uses of Special Operations Forces," Center for Strategic and International Studies, March 6, 2020.

[6] See, for example, Eric Robinson, "The Missing, Irregular Half of Great Power Competition," West Point Modern War Institute, September 8, 2020.

[7] DoD, 2022. ·

The deterrence-based aspects of this approach to campaigning are well understood by the U.S. military—warfighting capabilities are developed, exercised, and postured short of war to reduce the likelihood that a competitor will resort to military aggression to achieve their objectives. But the other half of this guidance—efforts to undermine and complicate competitors' efforts short of war—signal the need for new thinking about the military's strategic potential in competition. This builds upon growing discussion of the military's role in imposing costs,[8] creating dilemmas,[9] and targeting the vulnerabilities of rival states short of war.[10] While these terms are useful in their simplicity, they are insufficient on their own to explain how costs can be imposed, dilemmas created, and vulnerabilities targeted to generate positive strategic outcomes for the United States and not just unintended escalation in response.

This report, and its concept for strategic disruption, seeks to fill this void. The logic of this approach to strategic disruption is summarized in Figure 2.1.

FIGURE 2.1
The Logic of Strategic Disruption

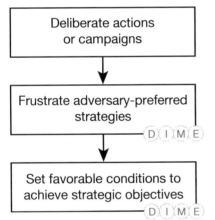

A friendly actor conducts deliberate actions or campaigns intended to frustrate an adversary's strategic or operational design.

These activities delay, degrade, or deny an adversary's ability to achieve core DIME interests (across the DIME spectrum) through their preferred courses of action, often by targeting vulnerabilities in the adversary's preferred approach.

These disruptive effects create time, space, and opportunities to achieve friendly strategic DIME objectives.

---

[8] See, as examples, Hal Brands and Tim Nichols, *Cost Imposition in the Contact Layer: Special Operations Forces and Great-Power Rivalry*, American Enterprise Institute, July 2021; Kenneth P. Ekman, *Winning the Peace Through Cost Imposition*, Brookings Institution, May 2014; Doowan Lee, "Cost Imposition: The Key to Making Great Power Competition an Actionable Strategy," West Point Modern War Institute, April 8, 2021; Brandon Valeriano, "Cost Imposition Is the Point: Understanding U.S. Cyber Operations and the Strategy Behind Achieving Effects," Lawfare, March 27, 2020.

[9] See, as examples, U.S. Army Training and Doctrine Command Pamphlet 525-3-1, *The U.S in Multi-Domain Operations, 2028*, U.S. Department of the Army, December 6, 2018; U.S. Army Training and Doctrine Command Pamphlet 525-3-1, *The U.S. Army Operating Concept: Win in a Complex World*, October 7, 2014; Curt Taylor and Larry Kay, "Putting the Enemy Between a Rock and a Hard Place: Multi-Domain Operations in Practice," West Point Modern War Institute, August 27, 2019.

[10] See, for example, Seth G. Jones, "The Future of Competition: U.S. Adversaries and the Growth of Irregular Warfare," Center for Strategic and International Studies, February 4, 2021; Taylor and Kay, 2019.

Strategic disruption begins when U.S. or friendly forces (in the top box of Figure 2.1) conduct individual tactical actions, or a series of tactical actions as part of an operational-level campaign, that are designed to frustrate some aspect of an adversary's preferred strategy to achieve their core national interests.

These disruptive actions do not seek to produce strategic effects in and of themselves. Rather they aim (in the middle box of Figure 2.1) to delay, degrade, or deny an adversary's ability to achieve any number of broader DIME interests. Specifically, these disruptive activities (or campaigns) seek to impose costs or create dilemmas that limit an adversary's ability to achieve their core interests through preferred courses of action. This often involves efforts by the friendly actor to target underlying vulnerabilities in the adversary's preferred approach. Implicit in this concept is that the adversary's preferred course of action is the one that it assesses as most likely to achieve their own strategic objectives.

Ultimately, strategic disruption frustrates an adversary's preferred strategy to (in the bottom box of Figure 2.1) create the time, space, and opportunities for the friendly government to leverage various tools—not just military ones—to achieve its own strategic objectives. This approach sets favorable conditions for the ultimate achievement of a strategic objective across the DIME spectrum, either in short order or over longer-duration campaigns.

An example helps to explain this logic. From 1956 to 1971, the U.S. Central Intelligence Agency (CIA) conducted a deliberate paramilitary campaign (the top box of Figure 2.1) to support Tibetan resistance fighters against Chinese Communist Party (CCP) occupation and rule.[11] These efforts degraded the ability of the CCP to assert the legitimacy of its rule over Tibet (the middle box of Figure 2.1) by forcing them to devote additional resources to consolidating local control contrary to their preferred approach. Ultimately, this campaign helped generate strategic diplomatic advantage (bottom box of Figure 2.1) for the United States by providing bargaining advantages during the Nixon administration's efforts to pursue a Sino-U.S. rapprochement in the early 1970s, exploiting the broader souring of Sino-Soviet relations at the time.

This classic example of unconventional warfare (UW) represents just one approach to strategic disruption explored throughout this report, but it neatly encapsulates the three foundational tenets of our concept—its proactive nature, its focus on frustrating adversary-preferred strategies, and its role in enabling effects across multiple instruments of national power.

Strategic Disruption Is Proactive

The first tenet of our broader concept for strategic disruption is that it is proactive in nature. By *proactive*, we mean that strategic disruption entails using military forces deliberately to set conditions that are favorable for the achievement of friendly strategic objectives. To use an

---

[11] U.S. Department of State, 1964; Dunham, 2004.

analogy, strategic disruption is more than just responding to an opponent's last move on the chess board. Instead, it is deliberately moving pieces across the board to constrain an opponent's options for their next move and frustrating their preferred strategy for victory. In this sense, strategic disruption still involves responding to an adversary's preferred approach or initial moves. But it is proactive because it seeks to get ahead of an adversary's ensuing moves, rather than reacting to each in isolation.

Despite the ongoing debate over whether the military's proper role in competition should simply be to prepare for war, a growing chorus of strategic guidance from DoD has signaled policy appetite for military forces to become more proactive in competition. The 2018 NDS's concept for dynamic force employment, for example, called for the Joint Force to "shape proactively the strategic environment" through "proactive and scalable employment of the Joint Force," to provide "national decision-makers with better military options."[12] The 2019 Irregular Warfare Annex to the NDS similarly directed efforts to "dictate the terms and tempo of competition to prevail against all global adversaries short of war, and build and sustain our global advantage."[13] More recently, the Chief of Staff of the Army's 2021 competition white paper cited the need for impede actions to "degrade adversary reputation, leverage, or advantage," direct competition to "enable Joint Force escalation superiority," and indirect competition to shape "adversarial behavior to better align with U.S. interests."[14] This language echoes the 2022 NDS's emphasis on undermining and complicating competitor coercion in calling for proactive, deliberate, and perhaps even offensive efforts to achieve U.S. objectives and frustrate adversary efforts prior to the onset of major hostilities.

Yet despite this demand signal, the U.S. military has often struggled to embrace a proactive approach to campaigning. Prior RAND Corporation research on Chinese and Russian gray zone behavior concludes, for example, that the United States frequently cedes the initiative when its competitors employ military coercion short of war, often because the U.S. military lacks a sufficient toolkit to respond without resorting to conventional force.[15] Take, for example, the United States' decision in 2013 to forgo using military force to enforce redlines in Syria related to the Assad regime's use of chemical weapons, primarily out of the fear of being drawn into a larger conflict. Adversary hostile activities short of war are frequently tailored to make a conventional military response by the United States appear risky or even disproportional in response. The result is that "contemporary discussions on great power competition are devoid of proactive, self-justified foreign policy options," leaving the United

---

[12] DoD, 2018b, p. 7.

[13] DoD, *Summary of the Irregular Warfare Annex to the National Defense Strategy,* 2020a, p. 1.

[14] U.S. Department of the Army, *The Army in Military Competition,* Chief of Staff Paper No. 2, March 1, 2021, p. v–vi.

[15] Lyle J. Morris, Michael J. Mazarr, Jeffrey W. Hornung, Stephanie Pezard, Anika Binnendijk, and Marta Kepe, *Gaining Competitive Advantage in the Gray Zone: Response Options for Coercive Aggression Below the Threshold of Major* War, RAND Corporation, RR-2942-OSD, 2019.

States to embrace a reactive posture that enables competitors to "dictate the time, place, and modality of competition" to their advantage.[16]

Ultimately, our concept for strategic disruption seeks to break this reactive cycle in future campaigning by articulating an approach to enabling broader strategic outcomes through the deliberate use of military forces in competition.

Strategic Disruption Seeks to Frustrate Adversary-Preferred Strategies

A second tenet of our definition of strategic disruption is that it seeks to frustrate adversary-preferred strategies. Specifically, we assess that strategic disruption requires deliberate efforts to delay, degrade, or deny an adversary's ability to achieve core interests via their own preferred courses of action.

Discussion on efforts to frustrate adversaries' preferred strategies often raises the potential to impose costs on an adversary. This approach seeks to "weaken a rival's ability to compete by disproportionately raising the costs—in time, energy, or resources—to achieve its objectives."[17] This highlights the essential time dimension of any military effort to complicate an adversary's strategic design and suggests that discrete efforts to disrupt an adversary are not likely to drive final, binary outcomes of success or failure in a campaign. Rather, strategic disruption efforts will often seek to delay an adversary's ability to achieve their objectives further into the future or simply degrade their ability to do so at present.

The Army's primary doctrine for SOF also highlights the role for disruption efforts to "induce conditions that influence a relevant actor to behave in a manner that is favorable for the joint force."[18] Specifically, it notes that "examples of these behaviors include making tactical or strategic decisions that make the relevant actor vulnerable to joint force lethal activities and taking actions that isolate the relevant actor from his center of gravity."[19] Existing doctrine for information operations (IO) and military deception cites a similarly forward-looking need to "disrupt, corrupt, or usurp the decision-making of our adversaries" and cause the adversary "to take specific actions (or inactions) that will contribute to the . . . friendly mission."[20] Prior analysis on subversion in the context of Cold War special operations also

---

[16] Bernard I. Finel, "Much Ado About Competition: The Logic and Utility of Competitive Strategy," West Point Modern War Institute, February 1, 2022.

[17] Brands and Nichols, 2021, p. 2.

[18] Army Doctrine Publication 3-05, *Army Special Operations*, U.S. Department of the Army, July 2019.

[19] Army Doctrine Publication 3-05, 2019.

[20] Joint Publication 3-13, *Information Operations*, U.S. Department of Defense, November 20, 2014, p. I-1; Joint Publication 3-13.4, *Military Deception*, U.S. Department of Defense, January 26, 2012, p. vii.

points to the strategic potential of subversive actions "designed to undermine the military, economic, psychological, or political strength or morale of a governing authority."[21]

These approaches all point to a common theme—efforts to frustrate adversaries' preferred strategies should look to interrupt an adversary's strategic or operational design by introducing new barriers in time, resources, or operational feasibility that complicate the adversary's ability to achieve their objectives through their preferred course of action. As a result, our concept for strategic disruption does not focus solely on denying or neutralizing an adversary's preferred approach, it also focuses on delaying or degrading their ability to leverage that approach to achieve their own core interests over time.

Strategic Disruption Enables Multiple Instruments of National Power

The final tenet of our concept for strategic disruption is that it sets favorable conditions for multiple instruments of national power to achieve strategic objectives—not just in the military domain but also in other aspects of statecraft across the DIME spectrum.[22] Implicit in this concept is that the initial deliberate operational activities or campaigning efforts to frustrate adversary-preferred strategies do not deliver strategic effects on their own. Rather, such efforts to interrupt an adversary's strategic or operational design through strategic disruption can create the time, space, and opportunities for various instruments of national power to achieve strategic outcomes themselves.

Most national strategies and existing research on strategic competition agree that nonmilitary tools have primacy over military tools in this space. As an example, the 2021 Interim National Security Strategic Guidance offered a "core strategic proposition" for how the United States should approach the modern security environment, placing nonmilitary instruments of power squarely in the lead:

> We will build back better our economic foundations; reclaim our place in international institutions; lift up our values at home and speak out to defend them around the world; modernize our military capabilities, while leading first with diplomacy; and revitalize America's unmatched network of alliances and partnerships.[23]

---

[21] U.S. Army Special Operations Command, "Unconventional Warfare Pocket Guide," April 5, 2016, p. 40.

[22] Recent years have seen the introduction of more varied versions of the DIME spectrum, such as MIDFIELD (military, informational, diplomatic, financial, intelligence, economic, law, and development) and DIMEFIL (diplomatic, informational, economic, financial, intelligence, and law enforcement). We focus on DIME because it remains the preferred delineation of instruments of power in Joint Publication 1-0, *Doctrine for the Armed Forces of the United States*, U.S. Department of Defense, July 12, 2017.

[23] White House, *Interim National Security Strategic Guidance*, March 2021, p. 3.

Regrettably, this emphasis on the relative strategic impact of nonmilitary capabilities in strategic competition has only increased calls for the military instrument of national power to leave competition to the rest of government and focus solely on deterring and preparing for war.[24] This logic is popular in part because it plays into legacy concerns within the U.S. military from perceived failures at interagency coordination in the counterinsurgency era; specifically, concerns that, although the military instrument of power was effective at clearing and holding territory in Iraq and Afghanistan, the United States was never fully able to consolidate its gains through nonmilitary efforts to stabilize these regions via development and diplomacy.[25] And yet, this argument ignores the complexities of fighting a modern counterinsurgency in unfamiliar territory,[26] as well as the significant historical legacy of military efforts to enable strategic effects in nonmilitary domains during prior periods of heightened tension between great powers short of war.[27] It also pins ultimate responsibility for strategic success on nonmilitary tools stepping in to fill voids created by the military instrument of power, rather than on military forces creating opportunities to capitalize upon preexisting advantages in nonmilitary domains of competition.

The 2022 NDS's concept for integrated deterrence provided a clearer vision for how military and nonmilitary instruments of national power could work in concert to maintain strategic advantages in competition. Undersecretary of Defense for Policy Colin Kahl, speaking in 2021, highlighted the need for such integration by noting,

> Our adversaries have developed theories of victory, cognizant that they wouldn't do particularly well in a protracted conflict with the United States. So they don't intend to fight a protracted conflict. Instead, they intend to blind us and deafen us and slow us down.[28]

To this effect, our concept for strategic disruption does not focus solely on the role for military forces in unilaterally disrupting the strategic aims of competitors. While that is cer-

---

[24] See, for example, Becca Wasser and Stacie L. Pettyjohn, "Why the Pentagon Should Abandon 'Strategic Competition'," *Foreign Policy*, October 19, 2021.

[25] See, for example, Nazanin Azizian, *Easier to Get into War Than to Get Out: The Case of Afghanistan*, Harvard University Belfer Center, August 2021.

[26] See, for example, Jason Lyall and Isaiah Wilson III, "Rage Against the Machines: Explaining Outcomes in Counterinsurgency Wars," *International Organization*, Vol. 63, No. 1, Winter 2009. Lyall and Wilson argue (p. 67) that "modern militaries possess force structures that inhibit information collection among local populations," making success in a counterinsurgency more difficult if the military force lacks preexisting understanding of the local operating environment.

[27] See, for example, Amy Ebitz, *The Use of Military Diplomacy in Great Power Competition: Lessons Learned from the Marshall Plan*, Brookings Institution, February 12, 2019; Fletcher Schoen and Christopher J. Lamb, "Deception, Disinformation, and Strategic Communications: How One Interagency Group Made a Major Difference," National Defense University Institute for National Strategic Studies, *Strategic Perspectives*, No. 11, June 2012.

[28] Jim Garamone, "Concept of Integrated Deterrence Will Be Key to National Defense Strategy, DOD Official Says," *Department of Defense News*, December 8, 2021.

tainly possible, it represents a high bar for the military instrument of power to achieve on its own in competition, particularly when most military capabilities are built to fight wars that involve open hostilities between rivals. Instead, strategic disruption focuses on the potential for military forces to create time, space, and opportunities for multiple instruments of national power to achieve strategic objectives through their own approaches.

To explore the military's potential to conduct strategic disruption that enables other instruments of national power, we leveraged the DIME construct throughout this report. These four instruments of national power—diplomatic, informational, military, and economic—provide a useful framework through which we explored how military forces can leverage strategic disruption to set conditions for "achiev[ing] national strategic objectives" outside the context of a major warfight.[29] Descriptions of those four instruments of national powers are as follows:

1. The **diplomatic instrument**—typically associated with the U.S. Department of State—is the "principal instrument for engaging with other states and foreign groups to advance US values, interests, and objectives, and to solicit foreign support for US military operations."[30]

2. The **informational instrument** is the creation, exploitation, and disruption of knowledge in support of strategic objectives.[31] It includes the "deliberate communication of specific information, on behalf of the government, to achieve a psychological effect that will influence behaviors, beliefs, and opinions in directions that support national policy and security."[32] It also includes the "ability to manipulate, deny, or destroy the information required for the decision making and basic functioning" of adversaries.[33]

3. The **military instrument**—the primary responsibility of DoD—focuses on the "use of force by one party in an attempt to impose its will on another . . . . [I]t can entail applying force, threatening the application of force, or enabling other parties to apply force in furtherance of strategic ends."[34]

4. The **economic instrument**, sometimes referred to as *economic statecraft*, "involves the use of economic instruments by a government to influence the behavior of another state."[35]

---

[29] Quoted from Joint Publication 1-0, 2017, p. I–12. See also, Joint Doctrine Note 1-18, *Strategy*, U.S. Department of Defense Joint Chiefs of Staff, April 25, 2018, p. II–5, II–8.

[30] Joint Publication 1-0, 2017, p. I–12.

[31] Joint Doctrine Note 1-18, 2018, p. II–6.

[32] Bethany C. Aragon, "Employing Information as an Instrument of National Power," U.S. Army War College, 2016, p. 2–3.

[33] Eric X. Schaner, "What Is Military Information Power?" *Marine Corps Gazette*, April 2020.

[34] Joint Doctrine Note 1-18, 2018, p. II–6.

[35] Jean-Marc F. Blanchard, Edward D. Mansfield, and Norrin M. Ripsman, "The Political Economy of National Security: Economic Statecraft, Interdependence, and International Conflict," *Security Studies*,

In our conceptual model for strategic disruption, efforts to frustrate an adversary's preferred strategy in one domain (e.g., economic) can create opportunities for achieving friendly strategic objectives in other domains. For example, disruptions to an adversary's economic strategy or operational approach can create openings for strategic military gains, and disruptions to an adversary's military strategic or operational design can create openings for diplomatic success. And while this report focuses on the military's role in strategic disruption, other nonmilitary tools—such as public diplomacy, sanctions, or development assistance— could also be used to frustrate an adversary's preferred strategies. In sum, strategic disruption campaigns can be conducted by multiple instruments of national power to frustrate adversaries' preferred strategies across multiple instruments of their national power, thereby setting favorable conditions to achieve strategic objectives across multiple friendly instruments of national power.

Vol. 9, Nos. 1–2, 2007, as cited in Jean-Marc F. Blanchard, Edward D. Mansfield, and Norrin M. Ripsman, eds., *Power and the Purse: Economic Statecraft, Interdependence and National Security*, Routledge, December 2013, p. 6.

CHAPTER 3

The Value Proposition of SOF in Strategic Disruption

This chapter and the remainder of this report explore the value proposition of SOF in strategic disruption.[1] SOF's strategic potential lies not in their unilateral military strength, which is limited relative to conventional military forces. Rather, we assessed SOF's value proposition in strategic disruption as their ability to frustrate adversary-preferred strategies through five unique pillars of capabilities—resist, support, influence, understand, and target—to create time, space, and opportunities to achieve strategic objectives across major elements of national power.

This chapter begins with a discussion of the theory and historical evolution of SOF as a strategic capability. We then introduce five core pillars of SOF capabilities for strategic disruption that are used in the remaining chapters of this report to explore the various mechanisms through which SOF can leverage strategic disruption to set conditions for strategic success across major elements of national power.

Theories of Special Operations' Strategic Potential

To understand the strategic potential of SOF for strategic disruption, it is important to first differentiate SOF capabilities and mission sets from other capabilities. A variety of different theories of special operations can help inform our assessment of SOF's specific value proposition in strategic disruption. Common themes include SOF's ability to present policymakers with options to influence politically sensitive portions of the world, to leverage highly specialized capabilities for unilateral and partnered operations, and to do so with reduced cost (in resources and risk) relative to a comparable deployment of other military forces.

Special operations are "activities or actions requiring unique modes of employment, tactical techniques, equipment, and training often conducted in hostile, denied, or politically

---

[1] The term *value proposition* was originally defined (in 1988) as "a clear, simple statement of the benefits, both tangible and intangible, that the company will provide, along with the approximate price it will charge each customer segment for those benefits." See Michael J. Lanning and Edward G. Michaels, "A Business Is a Value Delivery System," McKinsey Staff Paper No. 41, June 1988.

sensitive environments."[2] This description highlights two intrinsically unique aspects of SOF compared with most other military forces—SOF employ specialized approaches that require outsized investments in training and equipping compared with other forces, and SOF are designed to conduct missions in sensitive parts of the world likely to carry significant strategic risk to pursue strategic opportunities.

A larger body of research has sought to translate these two factors—SOF's unique capabilities and exquisite placement and access—into a generalizable theory of special operations that can help define the strategic potential of SOF as a broader tool of military power. One of SOF's core strengths is their ability to achieve outsized effects through speed and precision, such that "a successful special operation mission defies conventional wisdom by using a small force to defeat a much larger or well entrenched opponent."[3] SOFs other core strength is working with partner forces in areas that are denied or otherwise difficult for larger, conventional forces to access.[4] Such an approach to "build[ing] and fight[ing] alongside indigenous combat formations . . . provides the United States with an alternative to unilateral . . . efforts that typically produce long-term effects and potential political risk."[5] Expanding upon this logic, others have argued that,

> Special operations are most effective strategically when they are used in a sustained campaign to improve the performance of those forces primarily used in the conflict. In wars that have been more conventional in nature, special operations when used properly have improved the performance of conventional forces, increasing the strategic effectiveness of the latter. In contemporary irregular conflicts, special operations should be used to improve the performance of friendly host nation forces . . . proxy forces, or those interagency organizations which best address the underlying causes.[6]

The strategic utility of special operations can also be seen in the relative mismatch between the limited resources and small footprint required to conduct special operations missions, as compared with the ensuing costs in time and resources imposed upon adversaries as the result of such missions. This concept has been framed in a tactical sense as "relative superiority," or "a condition that exists when an attacking force, generally smaller, gains a decisive advantage over a larger or well defended enemy."[7]

---

[2] DoD, *DoD Dictionary of Military and Associated Terms*, November 2021, p. 199.

[3] William H. McRaven, "The Theory of Special Operations," Naval Postgraduate School, June 1993, p. 1.

[4] Charles T. Cleveland, James B. Linder, and Ronald Dempsey, "Special Operations Doctrine: Is It Needed?" *PRISM*, Vol. 6, No. 3, December 2016.

[5] Cleveland, Linder, and Dempsey, 2016, p. 12.

[6] James Kiras, "Special Operations and Strategies of Attrition," *Military Strategy Magazine*, Vol. 2, No. 4, 2012.

[7] McRaven, 1993, p.2.

Prior RAND research explores this asymmetry in the broader context of working through partner forces, arguing that the benefit of such asymmetry is in delivering asymmetric costs that "force opponents to spend disproportionate resources to defend against friendly capabilities."[8] From a campaigning perspective, this asymmetry also provides policymakers with sustainable long-term options to address political-military challenges that limit both fiscal risks (in terms of cost) and domestic political risks (in terms of the overall commitment of U.S. forces).[9] To similar effect, small-footprint special operations can generate outsized effects by enabling conventional military operations through targeting or exploiting the underlying sources of fog and friction in war that otherwise complicate military decisionmaking.[10]

These various theories of special operations can inform our assessment of SOF's specific value proposition in strategic disruption. Common themes include SOF's ability to present policymakers with options to influence politically sensitive portions of the world, to leverage highly specialized capabilities for unilateral and partnered operations, and to do so with reduced cost (in resources and risk) relative to a comparable deployment of other military forces.

Special Operations as a Strategic Enabler in Competition

Most of these theories of special operations, however, were designed to articulate SOF's strategic utility during armed conflict, primarily in the context of the United States' most recent experience fighting irregular wars against insurgents and violent extremist organizations (VEOs) in Iraq and Afghanistan. Given our focus on strategic disruption as a tool in strategic competition, it is important to understand whether SOF's strategic potential is different outside the confines of active hostilities.

There is a growing awareness that the role of SOF in strategic competition will need to change. Some have argued that SOF's future contributions are likely to resemble those made during the Cold War, focused on enabling various other elements of national power to achieve effects as part of "integrated statecraft solutions."[11] During the Cold War, SOF "demonstrated value in working through committed partners as a supplement for traditional deterrence."[12]

---

[8] Dan Madden, Dick Hoffmann, Michael Johnson, Fred T. Krawchuk, Bruce R. Nardulli, John E. Peters, Linda Robinson, and Abby Doll, *Toward Operational Art in Special Warfare*, RAND Corporation, RR-779-A, 2016, p. xv.

[9] Madden et al, 2016, p. xv.

[10] Robert G. Spulak Jr., *A Theory of Special Operations*, Joint Special Operations University Report 07-7, October 2007.

[11] Will Irwin and Isaiah Wilson III, *The Fourth Age of SOF: The Use and Utility of Special Operations Forces in a New Age*, Joint Special Operations University Report 22-1, 2022.

[12] Kevin Bilms, "Past as Prelude? Envisioning the Future of Special Operations," The Strategy Bridge, November 12, 2021.

SOF's value proposition may therefore be in their unique ability to remain persistently engaged in complex, contested environments to understand and exert U.S. influence.[13]

As a result, the strategic utility of special operations in competition will likely focus on its ability to deliver "short-term gains to increase the odds that long-term efforts can succeed," thereby setting the "conditions for the success of other instruments of national power."[14] Such an approach does not negate the lessons learned about the strategic utility of SOF as demonstrated during armed conflict—specifically SOF's ability to leverage indigenous forces in politically sensitive parts of the world with outsized impact on the enemy relative to the level of investment required by the United States. Rather, they point to SOF's strategic potential in competition to persuade "other human actors to conduct activities in concert with U.S. national objectives."[15]

SOF's ability to enable strategic effects across other elements of national power has been explored extensively in prior research. SOF, for example, can support the diplomatic instrument of national power via "long-term relationship building . . . [as the] folks we train end up being defense ministers and prime ministers and presidents";[16] as well as efforts to uncover adversary attempts to "destabilize critical regions, allies, or friends";[17] efforts to support conflict prevention by "enabling negotiations with and between adversaries, trust building, verification of agreements and crisis management";[18] and efforts to conduct "developmental and humanitarian projects" that can support U.S. diplomatic objectives.[19]

SOF can also support the informational instrument of national power by, for example, amplifying messages through tactical operations; "generating a positive image of the United States . . . [that] can create lasting impressions and incline the host-nation population to support the strategic goals of the United States"; supporting deterrence by either "displaying competence" through the deployment of specialized capabilities or by "advertising a capability that does not actually exist or is not fully developed"; and "providing access to remote or

---

[13] Bilms, 2021.

[14] Kiras, 2012.

[15] Field Manual 3-05.130, *Army Special Operations Forces Unconventional Warfare*, U.S. Department of the Army, September 2008, p. 2–11.

[16] Quote attributed to U.S. Senator Tim Kaine in U.S. Senate Armed Services Committee, "Part 5: Emerging Threats and Capabilities," in *Senate Hearing 113-465, Part 5*, U.S. Government Publishing Office, 2014.

[17] Linda Robinson, Todd C. Helmus, Raphael S. Cohen, Alireza Nader, Andrew Radin, Madeline Magnuson, and Katya Migacheva, *Modern Political Warfare: Current Practices and Possible Responses*, RAND Corporation, RR-1772-A, 2018, p. 308.

[18] Lars H. Ehrensvärd Jensen, "Special Operations: Myths and Facts," Royal Danish Defence College, 2014, p. 4.

[19] Steven Kashkett, "Special Operations and Diplomacy: A Unique Nexus," American Foreign Service Association, June 2017.

denied areas . . . [allowing] access to isolated or well-protected computer networks, important telecommunications nodes, or other information systems."[20]

SOF can support the larger military instrument of national power through efforts to train and enable local partner forces to deter aggression through asymmetric means, reducing the need for more-costly deployments of conventional forces as well as through efforts to conduct "operations to support priority missions in critical locations . . . to reduce strategic risk" and "facilitate integration with conventional forces during high-end conflict."[21]

SOF support to economic statecraft—which others have called economic warfare[22]—can include counter-threat finance efforts aimed at denying an adversary underlying sources of financial strength,[23] precision intelligence to support economic disruption,[24] or even indirect sabotage of economic infrastructure.[25]

Defining SOF's Value Proposition for Strategic Disruption

Strategic disruption, as defined in this report, sets favorable conditions to achieve national objectives through deliberate efforts to delay, degrade, or deny an adversary's ability to achieve core interests via their own preferred courses of action. Drawing from this analysis of SOF's strategic potential, we assessed that SOF's value proposition in strategic disruption is to frustrate adversary-preferred strategies through five unique pillars of capabilities—resist, support, influence, understand, and target—summarized in Table 3.1.[26]

---

[20] Mark Mitchell, "Strategic Leverage: Information Operations and Special Operations Forces," Naval Postgraduate School, 1999, p. 93–94, 95–96, 98.

[21] Christopher P. Maier, "Statement for the Record," opening statement, Committee on Armed Services, United States Senate hearing, April 5, 2022.

[22] Joseph L. Votel, Charles T. Cleveland, Charles T. Connett, and Will Irwin, "Unconventional Warfare in the Gray Zone," *Joint Forces Quarterly*, Vol. 80, No. 1, January 2016.

[23] Sara Dudley, Kevin D. Stringer, Steve Ferenzi, "Beyond Direct Action: A Counter-Threat Finance Approach to Competition," Kingston Consortium on International Security, 2021.

[24] David A Messenger, "'Against the Grain': Special Operations Executive in Spain, 1941–45," *Intelligence and National Security*, Vol. 20, No. 1, 2000; William Arkin and Robert Windrem, "The Other Kosovo War," MSNBC, August 29, 2001.

[25] David Kilcullen, "The Evolution of Unconventional Warfare," *Scandinavian Journal of Military Studies*, 2019.

[26] This framework is adapted from the U.S. Army Special Operations Command's (USASOC's) "Four Pillars of Capability," described in USASOC 2035. The four pillars include: (1) indigenous approach, (2) precision targeting, (3) understand & influence, and (4) crisis response. Specifically, we split "indigenous approach" into two components, given the increased importance of resistance as a component of SOF contributions to strategic competition. We also split "understand & influence" into its component parts, as shaping the attitudes of foreign actors (influence) is distinct from, albeit often dependent upon, efforts to extract strategically relevant information from politically sensitive or denied environments (understand).

TABLE 3.1

Five Pillars of SOF's Value Proposition in Strategic Disruption

Pillar	Definition	Primary SOF Activities
Resist	Efforts to enable a resistance or insurgency to coerce, disrupt, or overthrow a government or occupying power or deter an occupation.	UW
Support	Efforts to build the capacity of foreign security forces and enable their own efforts to defend against internal or external threats to their security.	Security force assistance, foreign internal defense, counterinsurgency, counterterrorism
Influence	Efforts to inform and shape the attitudes, behavior, and decisions of foreign actors in support of U.S. interests.	Civil affairs operations, military information support operations
Understand	Efforts to extract strategically relevant information from politically sensitive, contested, or denied environments.	Strategic reconnaissance
Target	Efforts to seize, destroy, disrupt, or secure key personnel, equipment, or infrastructure in politically sensitive, contested, or denied environments.	Direct action, hostage rescue, counter weapons of mass destruction

SOURCE: Adapted by authors from U.S. Army Special Operations Command, 2017; Joint Publication 3-05, *Special Operations*, U.S. Department of Defense, July 16, 2014.

The resist pillar of SOF's value proposition for strategic disruption focuses on efforts to enable a resistance or insurgency to coerce, disrupt, or overthrow a government or occupying power. These activities primarily focus on SOF's UW core activities but could also include efforts to prepare resistance forces in advance of conflict as a deterrent mechanism.

The support pillar focuses on efforts to build the capacity of foreign security forces and enable their own efforts to defend against internal or external threats to their security through means other than resistance. This includes a wider range of SOF core activities focused on working by, with, and through partner forces, including efforts to build the capacity of partners to defend against external threats (such as security force assistance), as well as efforts focused on supporting partners to deal with internal threats, including foreign internal defense, counterinsurgency, and counterterrorism.

The influence pillar focuses on efforts to shape the attitudes and behaviors of foreign actors to advance and support U.S. interests. This includes SOF core activities related to local governance and civic engagement through civil affairs operations, as well as the larger suite of military information support operations.

The understand pillar focuses on efforts to extract strategically relevant information from politically sensitive, contested, or denied environments. This includes SOF's core activity

For more on *USASOC 2035*, see U.S. Army Special Operations Command, "Communicating the ARSOF Narrative and Setting the Course to 2035," John F. Kennedy Special Warfare Center and School, 2017, p. 4–5.

focused on strategic reconnaissance, although understanding can also be gained as an incidental outcome of SOF efforts to conduct various other core activities.

Finally, the target pillar focuses on actions to seize, destroy, disrupt, or secure key personnel, equipment, or infrastructure in politically sensitive, contested, or denied environments. This pillar focuses primarily on SOF's direct action core activity but can also include hostage rescue activities and efforts to counter weapons of mass destruction to the extent both are focused on discrete actions against key personnel, equipment, or infrastructure.

Together, these five pillars represent the unique capabilities that SOF can leverage to frustrate an adversary's ability to achieve their core interests through their preferred courses of action. In the remaining chapters of this report, we explore historical examples in which SOF and SOF-like forces have leveraged each of these pillars to frustrate adversary-preferred strategies and produce strategic disruption. Specifically, we focused on identifying the various mechanisms through which SOF-led strategic disruption can create the time, space, and opportunities for major elements of national power to achieve strategic objectives.

Historical Analysis Approach

A few notes on our methodology for this historical analysis should be reiterated before we proceed into our pillar-specific analysis of SOF-led strategic disruption.

First, while we structured our analysis across each of these five pillars individually, most strategic disruption campaigns will, in practice, incorporate multiple pillars of this value proposition at once, given the interdependency of these components and the deliberate cross-functional nature of most special operations capabilities. Similarly, strategic disruption campaigns that enable strategic success in one domain of national power (e.g., diplomatic) may be likely to support strategic objectives in other domains as well (e.g., informational or economic). Our goal in this analysis was to extract a comprehensive set of the various mechanisms through which each pillar of strategic disruption can enable strategic effects across the DIME spectrum. As a result, our assignment of specific examples to one pillar over another was intended to be illustrative of these mechanisms and not exclusive of the potential for individual campaigns to employ multiple types of operational approaches (e.g. resistance and influence) to pursue strategic disruption.[27]

Second, our historical review drew not just on the experience of the United States in strategic disruption, but also on allied, partner, and even adversary actions. This approach does not imply our endorsement of the intent of specific adversary operations, nor that the United States should seek to replicate similar approaches. Rather, we aimed to draw out relevant les-

---

[27] In practice, this means that historical cases are highlighted in multiple chapters of our report, primarily when they offer unique evidence of additional mechanisms for strategic disruption across the DIME spectrum.

sons from how such disruptive activities were used to set conditions for the achievement of strategic outcomes.

Third, our historical analysis also included examples of strategic disruption conducted by *SOF-like units*, which we define as small teams of highly trained personnel with the mandate to affect conditions in politically sensitive or denied environments. This inductive approach was intended to capture relevant lessons from forces with similar specialized capabilities and mandates to operate in politically sensitive environments. Ultimately, most cases we analyzed were not drawn from the experience of U.S. SOF alone. This wider focus aimed to ensure that our concept for strategic disruption is inclusive not just of current capabilities within the SOF enterprise, but also other capabilities that could become more central to SOF's operational approach in campaigning in the future.

Fourth, despite this report's focus on the role for military forces in campaigning short of war, we did include historical examples of strategic disruption that can occur during conflict. Our aim was twofold. First, we looked to draw out the implications of such activities for analogous peacetime efforts to deter aggression in advance of conflict. Similarly, given Cold War precedents, we also acknowledged that strategic disruption during campaigning could include limited violence as part of indirect, proxy, or low-intensity confrontations between great powers but still remaining short of an all-out war.

Finally, it is worth reiterating that our goal was not to assess the efficacy of individual strategic disruption campaigns. Some were certainly a success; others were outright failures. Most were somewhere in between, and we describe these varied outcomes in some detail throughout the text. However, a detailed diagnosis of the exact attributes defining successful strategic disruption campaigns was not the focus of this research. Instead, our aim was more foundational—to explore the underlying logic of such campaigns and identify various mechanisms for how SOF can leverage disruption campaigns to enable friendly strategic success across the DIME spectrum. Identifying these mechanisms—and SOF's strategic potential to leverage strategic disruption in pursuit—is a critical first step toward eventual research that can empirically diagnose the drivers of success and failure in this unique space.

CHAPTER 4

The Resist Pillar of Strategic Disruption

We begin with the resist pillar of SOF's value proposition for strategic disruption, which involves efforts to enable a resistance or insurgency to coerce, disrupt, or overthrow an adversary government or occupying power or deter an occupation.[1]

SOF has primarily conducted such UW missions in wartime to help indigenous resistance movements defeat or degrade an adversary's government or to bring about the withdrawal of an adversarial government or foreign occupying force.[2] In situations of heightened tensions with a rival state short of outright war, resistance can also be used to impose more-limited costs, forcing opponents to spend disproportionate resources to defend against threats from internal actors supported by an external backer. It may also be used to coerce a change in policy of an incumbent regime, forcing an adversary to take actions it would not have otherwise been inclined to take.[3] In peacetime, support to resistance can also be used as an asymmetric tool for deterrence—for example, preparing resistance capacity in friendly countries could deter a hostile adversary from undertaking conventional aggression in the first place.[4]

Table 4.1 summarizes a set of historical examples in which resistance activities enabled strategic disruption. In the sections that follow, we review these historical vignettes to examine the mechanisms through which SOF (or SOF-like forces) pursued strategic disruption to enable friendly strategic outcomes across DIME dimensions of national power.

---

[1] This definition is based off a variety of sources, including Paul Tompkins, Joe Tonon, Erin Hahn, and Guillermo Puncczuk, "Unconventional Warfare Study Research and Writing Guide," U.S. Army Special Operations Command and the Johns Hopkins University Applied Physics Laboratory, undated; Department of Defense Directive 3000.07, *Irregular Warfare*, U.S. Department of Defense, May 12, 2017; Joint Publication 3-05, 2014.

[2] Madden et al., 2016.

[3] Madden et al., 2016; Votel et al., 2016.

[4] Otto C. Fiala, Kirk Smith, and Anders Löfberg, "Resistance Operating Concept (ROC)" Joint Special Operations University Press, 2020.

TABLE 4.1

Historical Examples of Resistance and Strategic Disruption

Dates	Program (Actor)	Target	Intended Disruptive Effect	Outcomes			
1941–1945	UW in Yugoslavia (SOE, OSS)	Axis Powers	Fix German and Italian conventional forces to prevent their employment in other theaters	D	I	**M**	E
1942	Detachment 101 (OSS)	Japan	Undermine perceptions of Japanese success in Burma using a proxy force	D	**I**	M	E
1944–1945	Operation Jedburgh (OSS)	Germany	Sabotage and harass German forces in occupied France, keep resistance leadership focused on Germany as common enemy	**D**	I	**M**	E
1956–1971	Tibetan Resistance (CIA)	China	Force China to commit additional resources to Tibet to maintain control	**D**	I	M	E
1979–1989	Mujahideen in Afghanistan (U.S.)	USSR	Impose costs and drain resources from the Soviet Union in the invasion of Afghanistan	**D**	**I**	**M**	E
1980–1992	Support to Lebanese Hezbollah (Iran)	Israel	Limit Israel's expansion into Lebanon and coerce Israel to withdraw its military forces from the country	**D**	I	**M**	E
2001	Support to Northern Alliance (U.S. SOF)	Taliban	Leverage indigenous partner forces as a primary means of overthrowing the Taliban regime in 2001	D	I	**M**	E
2003	Kurdish Peshmerga Forces (U.S. SOF)	Iraq	Leverage indigenous partner forces as a shaping effort in support of larger, conventional force operations	D	I	**M**	E
2013–2014	Propaganda Campaign in Eastern Ukraine (Russia)	Ukraine	Destabilize eastern Ukraine through propaganda and UW to prevent Kyiv from asserting authority over breakaway regions	D	**I**	**M**	E
2014–present	Build Baltic Total Defense Capacity (U.S.)	Russia	Build NATO and Baltic states' capacity for total defense in the event of a Russian occupation	**D**	I	**M**	E
2014–present	Fentanyl Crisis (China)	United States	Precipitate a drain on the U.S. economy and U.S. society by neglecting to constrain the proliferation of fentanyl precursors entering the U.S. via cartels	D	I	M	**E**

NOTE: OSS = Office of Strategic Services; SOE = Special Operations Executive; USSR = Union of Soviet Socialist Republics. Bold letters indicate that an example pursued friendly diplomatic (D), informational (I), military (M), or economic (E) outcomes.

Diplomatic Effects

The resist pillar of SOF's value proposition for strategic disruption can support diplomatic efforts in several ways, including by serving as a tool to bring about a change in an adversary's policy in ways that are advantageous to U.S. interests. For example, the CIA's support of a resistance movement in Tibet from 1956–1971 (with support from DoD) helped to provide modest political bargaining advantages for the United States as the Nixon administration pursued a Sino-U.S. rapprochement in the early 1970s, deepening the broader souring in Sino-Soviet relations at the time.[5] Additionally, even though U.S. government support to resistance in Afghanistan after the Soviet invasion in 1979 was initially intended to make the Soviet occupation more costly (as discussed later in this chapter), the eventual success of this support enabled the United States to expand its goals toward coercing the Soviet Union to eventually withdraw its military forces from Afghanistan entirely.[6] Iran's growing support to a foreign proxy in the 1980s similarly aimed to limit Israel's expansion into neighboring Lebanon by raising pressure on Israel to withdraw from that country.[7]

Resistance may also support diplomatic objectives for strategic disruption by helping to shape the character of resistance movements against adversaries and ensure their continued alignment with U.S. objectives and ability to frustrate adversary approaches. SOF's support can enable the success of a resistance movement by, for example, encouraging and facilitating the consolidation of disparate factions or thwarting the development of competing factions within a broader resistance movement. By ensuring that a resistance movement remains cohesive, SOF can enable the broader diplomatic objectives of keeping such movements focused on shared political objectives. While U.S. efforts to support resistance movements in occupied France during World War II (under Operation Jedburgh) are often credited for their operations to sabotage critical German infrastructure prior to D-Day, one of their primary successes was enabling the Allies to maintain broader cohesion across various factions within the wartime French political leadership. General Joseph Votel, former Commander of United States Special Operations Command (USSOCOM), described their diplomatic contributions as follows: "[W]ith all of their tactical and operational successes, the Jedburghs' greatest strategic contribution might have been in keeping the tenuous French Forces of the Interior coalition intact, making the Jeds truly warrior-diplomats."[8]

---

[5] Luke A. Wittmer, "Covert Coercion: A Formal Analysis of Unconventional Warfare as an Interstate Coercive Policy Option," Naval Postgraduate School, June 2013; U.S. Department of State, 1964; Dunham, 2004.

[6] Madden et al., 2016.

[7] Tompkins et al., undated.

[8] Votel et al., 2016, p. 4.

Informational Effects

At their core, resistance efforts aim to influence a population to challenge the authority of an adversary regime. The resist pillar of SOF's value proposition in strategic disruption can therefore enable strategic level effects in the information space by undermining the legitimacy of an adversary government or occupying power, thereby frustrating the adversary's ability to assert friendly narratives. For example, the OSS Detachment 101 worked through a local partner force behind enemy lines in Burma during World War II to undermine Japanese perceptions of the military success of their own occupying forces. In addition to collecting intelligence and identifying targets to support air strikes against Japanese military infrastructure in Burma, Detachment 101 produced and distributed black propaganda materials through a Burmese resistance force that depicted the "misery and desperation of the Japanese situation."[9] These efforts helped to provide an alternative narrative among Japanese forces serving in Burma, and back at home, to counter "the rosy picture of the war that Japanese propogandists fed their own citizens."[10] U.S. support to resistance fighters against the Soviet occupation in Afghanistan also enabled broader strategic effects in the information space, mainly by demonstrating the limitations of the Soviet military in defending against small formations of lightly armed mujahideen fighters. This had the larger strategic effect in the information domain of discrediting global perceptions of Soviet military power.[11]

In 2013 and 2014, Russian UW efforts in Ukraine's easternmost Donbas region and in Crimea also aimed to propagate messages that would resonate with the population of eastern Ukraine to foment opposition to the Ukrainian central government in Kyiv. Before entering Crimea and the Donbas region with its own "little green men," Russia leveraged an aggressive information campaign to stoke popular unrest by targeting "television, radio, and social media through the use of highly trained operatives, including 'hacktivists' and seemingly independent bloggers," as well as the "use of Russia Today television as a highly effective propaganda tool," and the "use of professional actors who portray themselves as pro-Russian Ukrainians."[12] This propaganda campaign—in combination with other irregular methods that generated military effects, such as the use of Russian SOF and a cyber campaign targeting critical infrastructure—helped Moscow frustrate the ability of the eventual pro-

---

[9] Daniel De Wit, "Fake News for the Resistance: The OSS and the Nexus of Psychological Warfare and Resistance Operations in World War II," *Journal of Advanced Military Studies*, Vol. 12, No. 1, Spring 2021, p. 48.

[10] De Wit, 2021, p. 48.

[11] Daria Fane, "After Afghanistan: The Decline of Soviet Military Prestige," *The Washington Quarterly*, Vol. 13, No. 2, Spring 1990.

[12] U.S. Army Special Operations Command, *Little Green Men: A Primer on Modern Russian Unconventional Warfare, Ukraine 2013–2014*, United States Army Special Operations Command and Johns Hopkins University Applied Physics Lab, undated, p. 44.

European government in Kyiv to assert legitimate authority over the Donbas region, complicating efforts for Kyiv to seek closer relations with the West.[13]

Military Effects

The resist pillar of SOF's value proposition for strategic disruption also contributes to the success of broader military campaigns. During an armed conflict, support to resistance can shape and enable broader operations by conventional forces to achieve operational and strategic effects in a campaign. For example, in the lead-up to the invasion of Iraq in 2003, a team of both CIA and SOF operatives worked with anti-Saddam Kurdish Peshmerga partner forces to perform "critical preparatory work for subsequent operations in northern Iraq" by 10th Special Forces Group.[14] U.S. military operations to enable Peshmerga resistance successfully prevented various Iraqi Army divisions from "reinforcing the defense of Baghdad or attacking the Coalition invasion force," ultimately enabling the broader military success of the invasion. [15] During World War II, the British SOE and the American OSS similarly conducted a resistance campaign in Yugoslavia through a guerilla element to enable Allied forces freedom to maneuver in other theaters. The resistance movement "effectively fixed in place 35 German and Italian divisions in the western Balkan region during 1941–1945," preventing their use in other theaters of the war and rendering them strategically irrelevant.[16] While our concept for strategic disruption focuses primarily on opportunities in strategic competition, there is potential for such support to resistance in a low-intensity conflict to fix adversary conventional forces in one theater, thereby limiting the likelihood they will engage in conventional aggression against more-vulnerable or strategically important areas.

Finally, resistance can also be an essential component of preparing a partner to respond to conventional aggression short of war, serving as an asymmetric deterrence option that shifts an adversary's cost-benefit calculus away from military intervention:

> An adversary contemplating the conquest and occupation of a territory, the population of which has already prepared to resist, may be deterred from attacking, knowing the presumed high cost of pacification the aggressor would have to pay.[17]

---

[13] Seth G. Jones, *Three Dangerous Men: Russia, China, Iran, and the Rise of Irregular Warfare*, W. W. Norton, 2021, p. 62-63.

[14] Andrew L., Mick Mulroy, and Ken Tovo, "Irregular Warfare: A Case Study in CIA and U.S. Army Special Forces Operations in Northern Iraq, 2002–3," Middle East Institute, August 2021.

[15] U.S. Army Special Operations Command, 2017, p. 6.

[16] J. Darren Duke, Rex L. Phillips, and Christopher J. Conover, "Challenges in Coalition Unconventional Warfare: The Allied Campaign in Yugoslavia, 1941–1945," *Joint Forces Quarterly*, No. 75, September 30, 2014, p. 129.

[17] Robert Haddick, *How Do SOF Contribute to Comprehensive Deterrence?* Joint Special Operations University Report 17-11, 2017, p. 62.

For example, after Russia's initial invasion of Crimea and aggression in eastern Ukraine in 2013 and 2014, the United States began efforts to "underscore the NATO alliance's resolve and improve its capabilities for resisting both conventional and irregular aggression" in the Baltic States, including efforts by U.S. SOF to conduct exercises, training, and joint deployments with Baltic and other European SOF partners focused on Allied defense and resistance.[18] This capacity-building effort aims to raise the costs of a potential Russian invasion of the Baltics by making it exceedingly difficult and painful.[19] It also supplements ongoing domestic efforts within the Baltic states for total defense against potential Russian aggression, defined as "a whole-of-society approach to national defense and resilience . . . designed to enhance deterrence by denial and by increasing the cost of aggression, while also supporting conventional defense efforts to counter and repel military attacks."[20]

Resistance can also be the main, essential military approach used in an irregular war. Efforts by U.S. SOF to link up with Northern Alliance militia fighters in Northern Afghanistan in late 2001 (as part of Task Force Dagger) directly enabled and precipitated the collapse of the Taliban regime in Afghanistan in 2001.[21] In strategic competition, such an approach could be used to deter opportunistic aggression or impose costs in secondary theaters in the event of heightened tensions between rival states (manifested through limited violence and proxy conflicts between such rivals).

Economic Effects

Finally, the resist pillar of SOF's value proposition for strategic disruption can be used as a cost imposition tool to economically weaken adversaries by draining an occupying power's resources over a prolonged period of time or preventing an opponent from expending resources against higher priorities. While the immediate targets of such disruption may often be military ones, this disruption can also produce economic effects when conducted at scale or over long durations, inducing a competitor to reconsider the fiscal and opportunity costs of a given course of action.

For example, U.S. policymakers initially viewed their support to resistance fighters against the Soviet occupation of Afghanistan as an opportunity to "enmesh the Soviets in

---

[18] Stephen Watts, Sean M. Zeigler, Kimberly Jackson, Caitlin McCulloch, Joe Cheravitch, Marta Kepe, *Countering Russia: The Role of Special Operations Forces in Strategic Competition*, RAND Corporation, RR-A412-1, 2021, pp. 38-39.

[19] Davis Winkie, "Less Door-Kicking, More Resistance: Inside Army SOF's Return to Unconventional Warfare," *Army Times*, September 9, 2021.

[20] Stephen J. Flanagan, Jan Osburg, Anika Binnendijk, Marta Kepe, and Andrew Radin, *Deterring Russian Aggression in the Baltic States Through Resilience and Resistance*, RAND Corporation, RR-2779-OSD, 2019, pp. 1–2.

[21] Elizabeth M. Collins, "First to Go: Green Berets Remember Earliest Mission in Afghanistan," U.S. Army Public Affairs, February 8, 2017.

a protracted conflict" and inflict on the Soviet Union their own Vietnam."[22] As Hal Brands and Tim Nichols noted: "[I]n the early 1980s, most U.S. officials had little expectation that the Afghan mujahideen could drive the Red Army out of Afghanistan, so the program's purpose was simply to bleed Soviet forces."[23] Indeed, RAND Arroyo Center analysis from the Cold War notes that the Soviet Union's military adventurism abroad "created a considerable drag on the civilian and military sectors of the economy," emphasizing the benefits to the United States of efforts to make it "as costly as possible for the Soviets to maintain or increase their empire."[24]

Similarly, the U.S. UW campaign in Tibet in the 1950s and 1960s was intended to "delay the consolidation of Chinese authority in Tibet" while "forc[ing] the Chinese to commit additional forces that might otherwise be free for other missions."[25] In both instances, support to resistance forces sought to drain an adversary government's time and treasure by bogging them down in a protracted conflict, not simply impose military costs.

Resistance can also undermine an adversary's economy by disrupting the foundations of its economic prosperity, even during competition. China's role in enabling the proliferation of fentanyl into the United States presents a nonstandard example of this approach, although not strictly a form of resistance in the doctrinal sense. Fentanyl, a critical component of the broader opioid epidemic, flows into the United States largely through transnational criminal organizations in Mexico that source precursor chemicals primarily from China.[26] This epidemic is not only a health crisis, but also a broader economic one, with estimates of the economic impact of the broader opioid epidemic at $504 billion (as of 2015) or roughly $1,672 per capita.[27] While Chinese leadership has made periodic pledges to reduce the ability of its domestic biopharmaceutical industry to export fentanyl precursors,[28] the U.S. Commission on Combating Synthetic Opioid Trafficking notes that Chinese leadership retains a "vested interest in allowing this industry to operate with little oversight or enforcement of regulation," given that it "contributes trillions of dollars each year to the PRC's economy."[29] While no evidence exists to suggest that China is deliberately leveraging the export of fentanyl into the United States through Mexican cartels as a cost imposition tool, its neglect of the prob-

---

[22] Madden et al., 2016, p. 112, 117.

[23] Brands and Nichols, 2021, p. 3.

[24] Charles Wolf, Jr., K. C. Yeh, Edmund Brunner, Jr., Aaron Gurwitz, Marilee Lawrence, *The Costs of the Soviet Empire*, RAND Corporation, R-3073/1-NA, 1984.

[25] Madden et al., 2016, p. 11; Brands and Nichols, 2021, p. 6–7.

[26] U.S. Commission on Combating Synthetic Opioid Trafficking, *Final Report*, February 2022, p. 5.

[27] Kaitlyn Hoevelmann, "The Economic Costs of the Opioid Epidemic," Federal Reserve Bank of St. Louis, September 4, 2019.

[28] U.S. Drug Enforcement Administration, *Fentanyl Flow to the United States*, Intelligence Report DEA-DCT-DIR-008-20, January 2020.

[29] U.S. Commission on Combating Synthetic Opioid Trafficking, 2022, p. 6–8.

lem to date not only imposes significant economic and social costs on its adversary but also enables China to pursue broader economic goals. Prior analysts have compared this dynamic with the role of Western states in the 19th century Opium Wars, leveraging the opium trade at the time "to exploit China economically and degrade its population and military power."[30]

---

[30] Ralph Little and Paul Pilliod, "Drug Warfare: The Confluence of Jihadist and China," North Florida High Intensity Drug Trafficking Areas Assessment 2017-1, August 2017, p. 9 as cited in John A. Pelleriti, Michael Maloney, David C. Cox, Heather J. Sullivan, J. Eric Piskura, and Montigo J. Hawkins, "The Insufficiency of U.S. Irregular Warfare Doctrine," *Joint Forces Quarterly*, No. 93, 2nd Quarter 2019, p. 107.

CHAPTER 5

The Support Pillar of Strategic Disruption

The support pillar of SOF's value proposition for strategic disruption involves building the capacity of foreign security forces and enabling their own efforts to defend against internal or external threats to their security. Through persistent and deliberate engagement, the support pillar of SOF's role in strategic disruption aims to build and enhance partner capabilities in such a manner that complicates competitors' strategic or operational design and enables other elements of national power to deliver strategic effects. SOF may perform a variety of activities with a partner force as part of this pillar of strategic disruption, including campaigning efforts to provide training, equipping, and institutional capacity-building to prepare for potential aggression from external threats, as well as efforts by SOF to provide advice and enablers to partner forces engaged in limited combat operations to address internal security threats.[1]

Support efforts by SOF can contribute to strategic disruption across the four elements of national power. Providing support to friendly government forces engaged in internal conflicts may provide the time and space to help a U.S. partner achieve a more favorable diplomatic settlement to a conflict or ongoing dispute short of war or deny an adversary the ability to achieve the same. Support may also help local partners to counter malign influence in competition as a tool to frustrate adversary-preferred strategies, or even develop the capability to conduct strategic IO themselves that promote friendly objectives in the information space. Assisting a partner to improve its military effectiveness may enhance deterrence by affecting the cost calculus of a potential adversary, who may decide that increased hostile activity again a strengthened partner force would not be worth the risk. Finally, SOF activities designed to support a partner force can help to set the conditions for U.S. economic development assistance to lock in long-term strategic gains in friendly countries, disrupting efforts by competitors to assert their influence or take advantage of instability.

Table 5.1 summarizes a set of historical examples in which support activities enabled strategic disruption. In the sections that follow, we review these historical vignettes to examine how SOF (or SOF-like forces) pursued strategic disruption to enable friendly strategic outcomes across DIME dimensions of national power.

---

[1] Robinson et al., 2019, p. 16.

TABLE 5.1

Historical Examples of Support and Strategic Disruption

Dates	Program (Actor)	Target	Intended Disruptive Effect	Outcomes			
1930s	Counter malign influence efforts in Latin America (FBI)	Nazi Germany	Enable nations in Latin America to identify and characterize Nazi influence efforts, empower anti-Nazi influences	**D**	**I**	M	E
1980–1992	Support to El Salvador against Communist insurgents (U.S. SOF)	USSR	Prevent defeat of US-friendly regime and achieve negotiated settlement to civil war	**D**	I	**M**	E
1983–1989	QRHELPFUL project (CIA)	USSR	Support the development of a partner's strategic IO capability, deny adversary control over political and information environment	**D**	**I**	M	E
1999–2007	U.S. SOF support to Plan Colombia (U.S. SOF)	FARC, counter-narcotics	Set conditions for U.S. economic assistance to enable long-term development through military operations	**D**	I	M	**E**
2001–2014	Operation Enduring Freedom—Philippines (U.S. SOF)	VEO	Reduce transnational terrorist threat and support for threat groups in the Philippines, professionalize and develop partner forces, enhance bilateral relationship	**D**	I	**M**	E
2003–Present	Build Iraq's CTS capability (U.S. SOF)	VEO	Enable CTS to maintain internal stability in Iraq, promote multi-ethnic Iraqi security institutions as a counterweight to sectarian influences	**D**	**I**	**M**	E
2014–2022	Security Sector reform in Ukraine (U.S.)	Russia	Counter-Russian efforts to degrade Ukrainian government and military effectiveness through malign influence and corruption	**D**	**I**	**M**	E
2015–2019	Support to pro-regime forces in Syria (Russia)	Anti-Assad forces	Deny anti-Assad forces a military victory, maintain access and influence for power projection	**D**	I	**M**	E

NOTE: CTS = counterterrorism service; FARC = Revolutionary Armed Forces of Colombia; FBI = Federal Bureau of Investigation; IO = information operations. Bold letters indicate that an example pursued friendly diplomatic (D), informational (I), military (M), or economic (E) outcomes.

Diplomatic Effects

The support pillar of SOF's value proposition for strategic disruption might create the time and space required to help partners secure a favorable diplomatic settlement in an internal conflict, irregular war, or militarized dispute short of conventional war. It could also deny adversaries the ability to achieve the same outcome. Prior RAND Arroyo Center analysis of limited-footprint U.S. military operations (including those conducted by SOF) provides considerable evidence that support from "small numbers of U.S. forces are associated with a partner government's ability to secure a negotiated settlement, even if they seldom help to achieve outright military victory."[2] Limited advisory support to a partner nation facing an internal threat can be effective even when a rival great power is providing military assistance to stoke that internal threat.[3]

For example, U.S. support in the form of a small number of trainers and advisers to the government of El Salvador against the Farabundo Martí National Liberation Front (FMLN) helped to prevent the defeat of El Salvador's government's forces in the 1980s, weaken the FMLN insurgency, and ultimately helped lead to a negotiated settlement to the conflict that helped prevent the spread of Soviet influence in Latin America during the Cold War.[4] Stated simply, SOF created the time and space for a weaker partner to secure a better deal.[5]

The support pillar of SOF's value proposition for strategic disruption may also contribute to U.S. diplomatic objectives by influencing a partner's preferences and encouraging greater alignment with U.S. interests and values. Through frequent, long-term interactions with partners, SOF may be able to influence partners' preferences and behavior on norms such as civilian control of the military and respect for human rights.[6] These efforts can frustrate adversary efforts to create divisions between the United States and potential partner nations or enable the United States to support partners to conduct operations that frustrate adversary-preferred strategies directly.

As an example, U.S. SOF advising partner security forces in the Philippines emphasized an approach to counterterrorism that "laid the groundwork for Philippine security forces to adopt an approach that minimized civilian harm as they pursued terrorist elements . . . the U.S. ethos was transferred to Philippine forces during close partnering efforts."[7] These efforts to professionalize the Philippine security forces since 2001 have enabled continued close relations between the two nations' militaries despite growing Chinese efforts to drive a wedge.[8]

U.S. SOF's capacity-building efforts with the Iraqi CTS, particularly SOF's focus on building a more inclusive and nonsectarian force compared with other parts of Iraq's security services, similarly contributed to broader U.S. diplomatic goals of building Iraqi security

---

[2] Watts, Noyes, and Tarini, 2021, p. 49.

[3] Watts, Noyes, and Tarini, 2021, p. 49.

[4] Madden et al., 2016, p. 98.

[5] Walter C. Ladwig, "Influencing Clients in Counterinsurgency: U.S. Involvement in El Salvador's Civil War, 1979–92." *International Security*, Vol. 41, No. 1, Summer 2016, p. 133.

[6] Alexandra Gheciu, "Security Institutions as Agents of Socialization? NATO and the 'New Europe,'" *International Organization,* Vol. 59, No. 4, Fall 2005, p. 974; Carla Martinez Machain, "Exporting Influence: U.S. Military Training as Soft Power," *Journal of Conflict Resolution*, Vol. 65, Nos. 2–3, 2020.

[7] Larry Lewis and Sarah Holewinski, "Changing of the Guard: Civilian Protection for an Evolving Military," *PRISM*, Vol. 4, No. 2, December 2013.

[8] For discussion, see Ralph Jennings, "Changing of the Guard: Civilian Protection for an Evolving Military," *PRISM*, Vol. 4, No. 2, December 2013.

institutions that were seen as legitimate by broad swaths of Iraq's multi-ethnic society.[9] The CTS's combat successes and ensuing popular support during efforts to retake Iraqi territory from the Islamic State helped frustrate Iranian efforts to wield predominantly Shia Popular Mobilization Units to similar effect. To this effect, U.S. SOF efforts to build a more inclusive and less sectarian security service made the CTS "a natural partner in blunting the influence of Iran" and "a reliable force that decreases Iraq's dependence on Iranian-directed Shi'a militia."[10]

Informational Effects

The support pillar of SOF's value proposition for strategic disruption can also help a partner build the capacity to conduct offensive influence and messaging activities against a shared competitor, expanding the ability of an external power to frustrate adversary objectives and enable broader strategic outcomes in denied or contested information domains. For example, from 1983 to 1989, the CIA helped the Polish Solidarity Movement develop the capacity to conduct strategic information operations aimed at delegitimizing Soviet influence in Poland, frustrating Soviet efforts to forcibly suppress Poland's democratic opposition and labor union movements. As part of the CIA's QRHELPFUL program, the United States provided material assistance to Solidarity in the form of "leaflets, posters, offset presses, Xerox machines, duplicators, typewriters, paper, and technical help in running clandestine radio broadcasts and breaking into television programs."[11] The immediate effect of this program was to undermine the ability of the Soviet Union to suppress Solidarity's influence, simultaneously enhancing the reach of pro-democracy and anti-Soviet messaging within Poland. Over the long term, this program helped set favorable conditions in Poland for democratic elections, and the eventual collapse of the Soviet Union.

Support activities can also help partners counter malign influence from adversaries, denying adversaries the potential to foment internal instability in the information domain through increased resilience. For example, SOF and SOF-like forces can help local partners to identify malign actors operating in their country and map their influence networks, as well as build the capacity of partner nations to act to degrade such networks. For example, in the lead-up to World War II, the FBI conducted operations in Latin America to counter influence networks developed by Nazi Germany. In Brazil, the FBI "created false identities that gave them access to areas with heavy Nazi influence" and "mapped in detail the identities and

---

[9] Michael Knights and Alex Mello, "The Best Thing America Built in Iraq: Iraq's Counter-Terrorism Service and the Long War Against Militancy," *War on the Rocks*, July 19, 2017.

[10] Watts, Noyes, and Tarini, 2021, p. 36–37.

[11] Seth G. Jones, "Going on the Offensive: A U.S. Strategy to Combat Russian Information Warfare," Center for Strategic and International Studies, October 2018b; Seth G. Jones, *A Covert Action: Reagan, the CIA, and the Cold War Struggle in Poland*, W. W. Norton, 2018a.

behaviors of active German agents while identifying government officials or prominent citizens who shared anti-Nazi sentiment."[12] This assistance enabled Brazilian authorities to chip away at and dismantle Nazi networks within the country, denying Berlin the ability to leverage Brazil as a tool to contest American influence and access within the Western Hemisphere.

Military Effects

The support pillar of SOF's value proposition for strategic disruption can also build the military effectiveness of partner forces to address shared military threats, thereby promoting the military benefits of close relations between a nation and its partners that advance shared interests. For example, Russia's military support to its long-standing Syrian partner, the Assad regime, helped Russia maintain its military presence and power projection ambitions in Syria and the broader Middle East against internal threats to the Assad regime's solvency.[13] Beginning in 2015, Russia enabled pro-regime forces throughout Syria to retake territory, often with advice and assistance from Russian Spetsnaz special forces units and private military contractors (PMCs) (such as Wagner Group) on the ground—providing training and facility security and enabling air support.[14] Russia's support "saved the Assad regime" and facilitated the government's control of most major Syrian cities, thereby promoting the military benefits of a close partnership with Russia to other potential partner states "without its forces becoming engaged in a quagmire."[15] Moreover, this support frustrated the ability of anti-Assad forces to leverage a military victory over the Assad regime to secure his removal from power, pushing future negotiations into the diplomatic realm where they were less likely to succeed and more likely to bolster Russia's reputation as an essential diplomatic powerbroker in the region (its core strategic priority for intervention).

The benefits of support activities on military relationships among partners are also seen in the long-term U.S. support of the Philippine armed forces for counterterrorism purposes. The endurance of these relationships meant that "many Philippine officers who served in SOF units and formed close ties with U.S. SOF ascended to senior levels in the armed forces and defense ministry."[16] This provided an opportunity for U.S. SOF to have greater influence on the Philippine military and "contributed to an overall enhancement of the U.S-Philippine military and overall bilateral relationship."[17] As in diplomatic competition, these

---

[12] Brands and Nichols, 2021, p. 6.

[13] Jones, 2021, p. 64–66.

[14] Mark Galeotti, "The Three Faces of Russian Spetsnaz in Syria," *War on the Rocks*, March 21, 2016.

[15] Jones, 2021, p. 72.

[16] Linda Robinson, "The SOF Experience in the Philippines and the Implications for Future Defense Strategy," *PRISM*, Vol. 6 No. 3, December 7, 2016, p. 161.

[17] Robinson, 2016, p. 158.

support efforts have enabled continued close military relations between the Philippines and the United States, frustrating Chinese efforts to drive a wedge.[18]

Support efforts can also build the capacity of partner forces to degrade internal security threats of mutual concern, enabling strategic disruption of adversary efforts to destabilize or impose costs against partner states and promoting enhanced internal stability as a result. For example, U.S. security sector assistance to the Ukrainian military after Russia's 2014 invasion of Crimea and aggression in eastern Ukraine sought to reduce corruption in Ukraine's defense industry.[19] This assistance limited the effectiveness of Russian efforts to "weaponize" corruption in Ukraine as a means of gaining influence and reducing the effectiveness of its military forces to fight back against Russian aggression.[20] Support to partner militaries can help those militaries be more independent, more nonpartisan, and less prone to coups or corruption—and therefore less susceptible to competitors' malign influence efforts.[21]

Economic Effects

The support pillar of SOF's value proposition for strategic disruption can also contribute to U.S. economic objectives by setting the conditions required for economic development assistance to take effect, delivering long-term strategic benefit to the United States and its partners. In Colombia, beginning in the late 1990s, U.S. SOF support to Colombian security forces contesting the FARC helped to create partner units capable of effectively combating insurgents and drug traffickers throughout Colombia.[22] Broader U.S. policy toward Colombia was encapsulated under Plan Colombia—an expansive list of policy proposals covering domestic political, social, economic, and military challenges in the country. By enabling Colombian forces to secure and stabilize their own territory through military efforts to disrupt drug trafficking and insurgent groups, SOF helped set the conditions in which broader U.S. economic and development assistance could achieve their greatest effects over many years, eventually transforming Colombia into a "lynchpin of security and prosperity in South

---

[18] For discussion, see Ralph Jennings, "Why the Philippines Picked America over China," Voice of America (VOA), August 5, 2021.

[19] Olga Oliker, Lynn E. Davis, Keith Crane, Andrew Radin, Celeste Ward Gventer, Susanne Sondergaard, James T. Quinlivan, Stephan B. Seabrook, Jacopo Bellasio, Bryan Frederick, Andriy Bega, and Jakub Hlavka, *Security Sector Reform in Ukraine*, RAND Corporation, RR-1475-1-UIA, 2016; Andrew Radin, "Chapter 6: Defense Reform in Ukraine," *Institution Building in Weak States*, Georgetown University Press, 2020.

[20] Karolina MacLachlan, "Corruption as Statecraft: Using Corrupt Practices as Foreign Policy Tools," Transparency International: Defense and Security, November 18, 2019.

[21] Stephen Watts, Alexander Noyes, and Gabrielle Tarini, *Competition and Governance in African Security Sectors: Integrating U.S. Strategic Objectives*, RAND Corporation, RR-A567-1, 2022, p. 22.

[22] Austin Long, Todd C. Helmus, S. Rebecca Zimmerman, Christopher M. Schnaubelt, and Peter Chalk, *Building Special Operations Partnerships in Afghanistan and Beyond: Challenges and Best Practices from Afghanistan, Iraq, and Colombia*, RAND Corporation, RR-713-OSD, 2015, p. 59.

America."[23] SOF's contributions to strategic disruption can therefore help lock in strategic gains in partner countries through economic approaches, negating the effectiveness of adversary efforts to leverage local instability to gain advantage.

---

[23] Quote attributed to Former Secretary of Defense Robert Gates, April 15, 2010, as cited in U.S. Global Leadership Coalition, "Plan Colombia: A Development Success Story," 2017.

CHAPTER 6

The Influence Pillar of Strategic Disruption

The influence pillar of SOF's value proposition for strategic disruption involves informing and shaping the attitudes, behavior, and decisions of foreign actors in support of U.S. interests.[1] Rather than frustrate adversary strategic or operational design through physical acts, influence activities often directly seed cognitive effects into the information environment that delay, degrade, or deny an adversary's ability to achieve their core interests using their preferred approach.

Influence efforts contribute to strategic disruption across the four elements of national power. In the diplomatic realm, influence contributions to strategic disruption may bolster the legitimacy of a state and its partners or, conversely, damage or degrade the reputation or legitimacy of an opponent on the world stage. It may also help to cement adherence to diplomatic initiatives through targeted information operations. In the information domain, influence can be used to lock in support from foreign populations during campaigning as a way to frustrate an adversary's preferred narratives. During both wartime military operations and preconflict deterrence, influence may be used to deceive or disorient hostile groups, to demoralize their forces, or to undermine the adversary's will to resist supporting broader military objectives. Influence contributions to strategic disruption may also be used during a military campaign to inform, unite, and sustain the support of neutral or friendly groups.[2] In the economic domain, influence efforts may set the conditions for economic assistance and investment to lock in support for the United States at the expense of an adversary.

Table 6.1 summarizes a set of historical examples in which influence activities enabled strategic disruption. In the sections that follow, we review these historical vignettes to examine how SOF (or SOF-like forces) pursued strategic disruption to enable friendly strategic outcomes across DIME dimensions of national power.

---

[1] Eric V. Larson, Richard E. Darilek, Daniel Gibran, Brian Nichiporuk, Amy Richardson, Lowell H. Schwartz, and Cathryn Quantic Thurston, *Foundations of Effective Influence Operations: A Framework for Enhancing Army Capabilities*, RAND Corporation, MG-54-A, 2009.

[2] Alfred H. Paddock, Jr, "Military Psychological Operations," in Carnes Lord and Frank R. Barnett, eds., *Political Warfare and Psychological Operations: Rethinking the U.S. Approach*, Washington, D.C.: National Defense University Press, 1989, p. 45.

TABLE 6.1

Historical Examples of Influence and Strategic Disruption

Dates	Program (Actor)	Target	Intended Disruptive Effect	Outcomes
1920s	The Trust (USSR)	Anti-Communist monarchists ("Whites")	Undermine political-military capabilities of Russian counterrevolutionaries; deceive Western intelligence agencies about USSR's strength	**D** **I** **M** E
1944	Operation SAUERKRAUT (OSS)	Germany	Undermine morale of German forces in Italy	D I **M** E
1948	VOA in Italy (U.S.)	Soviet Union	Set conditions for economic assistance and investment at the expense of Soviet influence	**D** **I** M **E**
1949–1972	RFE/RL (CIA)	Soviet Union	Constrain Soviet power by supporting anti-Communist elements in democracies at risk of takeover or weakening by the Soviet Union	D **I** M E
1950–1953	PSYOP in Korean War (U.S. Army)	North Korea	Degrade North Korea's will to fight; bolster the morale of Korean civilians	D I **M** E
1952–1961	Project LC-CASSOCK (CIA)	East Germany	Weaken and degrade Communist sentiment in East Germany	**D** **I** M E
1983–1987	Operation Denver (KGB, Stasi)	United States	Degrade international reputation of the United States through misinformation about origins of the HIV virus	**D** **I** M E
1995–1999	Joint Commission Observer in Bosnia (U.S. SOF)	Bosnian War combatants	Enforce the Dayton Accords by shaping local opinions in favor of the peace accord; establish the credibility of NATO's peacekeeping force	**D** I **M** E
2011–2017	Observant Compass (U.S. SOF)	LRA	Induce fighters to defect from the LRA	D I **M** E
2020	COVID-19 propaganda (China)	United States	Degrade international reputation of the United States through misinformation about origins of the COVID-19 pandemic and U.S. pandemic response	**D** **I** M E

NOTE: COVID-19 = coronavirus disease 2019; HIV = human immunodeficiency virus; KGB = Committee for State Security of the Soviet Union; NATO = North Atlantic Treaty Organization; PSYOP = psychological operation; RFE/RL = Radio Free Europe/Radio Liberty. Bold letters indicate that an example pursued friendly diplomatic (D), informational (I), military (M), or economic (E) outcomes.

Diplomatic Effects

The influence pillar of SOF's value proposition for strategic disruption may damage or degrade the reputation or legitimacy of an opponent, often to render them less effective as a political counterweight and create space for friendly goals to be achieved. For example, the 1920s Soviet influence operation codenamed "The Trust" was aimed at subverting the reputation and political strength of anti-Communist monarchists living abroad and in Russia after the Russian revolution. The Bolshevik secret police set up a fake organization to lull monarchists—who sought to reinstate the Tsarist monarchy in Russia—into complacency or convince them to return to Russia where they could be arrested. The influence operation "inflicted incalculable damage on the Russian emigres, undercutting their political and military capabilities to the point of rendering the counterrevolutionaries insignificant."[3] In terms of their ultimate strategic benefit, these efforts helped buy time and space for the nascent Soviet government to cement its early hold on power.

Operation Denver—a KGB misinformation campaign that sought to pin the emergence of the HIV virus on biological warfare research carried by U.S military scientists at Fort Detrick in Maryland—similarly sought to tarnish the reputation of the United States abroad, thereby creating openings for Soviet influence to grow as a result.[4] China's propaganda efforts in the early months of the COVID-19 pandemic—which included sending text messages to U.S. citizens falsely claiming that the military would enforce a quarantine, spreading rumors that the virus had originated in a U.S. military lab, and forging a memorandum from the commander of the USS *Theodore Roosevelt*—aimed to sow instability within the United States and reduce its support abroad by casting the United States as unable to manage the pandemic within its own borders and responsible for the pandemic in the first place. [5] In the future, similar influence efforts could create diplomatic openings for China to be seen as the more responsible party in international affairs.

Influence efforts by SOF may also help cement adherence to diplomatic initiatives through targeted information operations, thereby disrupting adversary efforts to sow instability. For example, during peacekeeping operations in the Balkans in the 1990s, U.S. SOF influence activities helped to enforce the 1995 Dayton Peace Accords, painstaking peace negotiations shepherded by U.S. diplomats which had put an end to the Bosnian War. U.S. SOF built out an influence network of local actors throughout Bosnian society that allowed the United States to "influence and act on problems" that threatened the peace agreement. U.S. SOF "co-opted bus company presidents and got to know criminal elements, both of which had a hand in the violence and could become a powerful force in stopping future violence."[6] This influence network helped to create options for commanders and policymakers as they attempted to enforce a diplomatic initiative of high priority to the United States and NATO.[7] During this time, the U.S. Army also implemented a "three-part information campaign that included a public information campaign to establish NATO credibility with international media, a PSYOP campaign to shape local opinions in favor of peacekeepers, and a civil-military coop-

3 Thomas Rid, *Active Measures: The Secret History of Disinformation and Political Warfare*, Farrar, Straus, and Giroux, 2020, p. 31–32.

4 Mark Kramer, "Lessons from Operation 'Denver,' the KGB's Massive AIDS Disinformation Campaign," MIT Press Reader, May 26, 2020.

5 Jones, 2021a, p. 1–3, 130–131.

6 Charles T. Cleveland and Daniel Egel, *The American Way of Irregular War: An Analytical Memoir*, RAND Corporation, PE-A301-1, 2020, p. 103.

7 Cleveland and Egel, 2020, p. 102.

eration campaign to provide factual information about civil-military relations between coalition forces and local government."[8]

Collectively, these efforts leveraged SOF's influence pillar of capability to frustrate and disincentivize local threat actors from conducting further ethnic violence, thereby increasing adherence to a broader diplomatic priority for the United States.

Informational Effects

The influence pillar of SOF's value proposition for strategic disruption can also be used to lock in support from foreign populations during campaigning as a way to frustrate an adversary's preferred narratives. During the Cold War, for example, the United States waged a strategic influence campaign to constrain the messaging power of the Soviet Union through the use of RFE/RL and VOA. These influence initiatives used short-wave radio stations to produce and spread content that aimed to "keep alive hope of a better future among the populations of the Soviet orbit, broaden the boundaries of internal debate within the USSR and Eastern Europe, encourage peaceful change, and make the Soviet empire [appear] as a less formidable adversary."[9] Collectively, these disruptive campaigns helped set favorable conditions for the eventual decline of the Soviet Union, and successful embrace of U.S. soft power by Eastern European nations in the 1990s.

The United States has also used other influence methods, such as black propaganda and forgeries, during the Cold War to tamp down or render ineffective Communist sentiment behind the Iron Curtain. For example, one of the CIA's "most prolific, innovative, and aggressive forgery factories of the entire Cold War" was Project LC-CASSOCK, an operation to "weaken or destroy Communist manifestations" in East Germany primarily in the 1950s.[10] The CIA used an advertisement and public relations firm in West Berlin to produce falsified editions of official East German publications—along with a significant logistics mechanism to distribute them. The publications were targeted at highly specific audiences that the CIA saw as traditionally less accessible to Western influence, such as the People's Police or the Socialist Party's youth organization.[11]

[8] Watts, Noyes, and Tarini, 2021, p. 64.

[9] A. Ross Johnson, "Managing Media Influence Operations: Lessons from Radio Free Europe/Radio Liberty," *International Journal of Intelligence and Counterintelligence*, Vol. 31, No. 4, December 20, 2018, p. 681–701.

[10] Rid, 2020, p. 85–86.

[11] Rid, 2020, p. 88–89.

Military Effects

The influence pillar of SOF's value proposition for strategic disruption can also be used to deceive adversaries about the strength of military forces, leading them to take actions they would not otherwise take if they had an accurate assessment of the capabilities. For example, another objective of the USSR's Operation Trust was to "deceive Western intelligence agencies about the military strength of the young and fragile Soviet Union."[12] The fake monarchist organization created by the USSR's secret police fed doctored material to Polish, Estonian, and Finnish intelligence services, who were then "keen to pass on what they considered valuable intelligence to their much more formidable Western counterparts" in France, Britain, Italy, and even the United States.[13] The goal of the operation was to convince various Western intelligence services to believe an exaggerated notion of the Red Army's military power and lead them to reject any option for military intervention against the newly formed USSR.

The influence pillar of SOF's value proposition for strategic disruption may also undermine the morale of adversary forces during conflict, potentially leading them to perform worse than they otherwise would have without such interventions. During World War II, the Morale Branch of the OSS conducted Operation Sauerkraut, an influence operation to attack the morale of German troops. The OSS recruited German and Czech prisoners of war (POWs) from Allied POW camps and dispatched them behind enemy lines to "circulate rumors, fake orders, and leaflets about growing unrest among German military leaders."[14] The influence operation also demoralized German troops by printing forged leaflets that led soldiers to believe that "the German wives and girlfriends they left behind were having casual affairs with foreign men."[15] During Operation Observant Compass throughout Central Africa from 2011 to 2017, U.S. SOF partnered with various nongovernmental organizations, United Nations peacekeepers, and African military forces in an effort to defeat the Lord's Resistance Army (LRA). The broader effort included an influence operation that aimed to encourage LRA soldiers to defect, primarily through the use of radio programming and a leaflet distribution campaign.[16] Similarly, PSYOPs during the Korean War provided support to military operations by using loudspeakers, radio, and leaflets to induce enemy soldiers to surrender and to bolster the morale of Korean civilians.[17] While these examples are drawn from armed conflicts, they could provide a template for SOF to leverage influence capabilities to achieve

---

[12] Rid, 2020, p. 25.

[13] Rid, 2020, pp. 27,31.

[14] CIA, "Barbara Lauwers: Deceiving the Enemy," webpage, August 19, 2019.

[15] CIA, "The 'Glorious Amateurs' of OSS: A Sisterhood of Spies," webpage, April 6, 2022.

[16] Jared M. Tracey, "A Team Approach: PSYOP and LRA Defection in 2012," *Veritas Journal of Army Special Operations History*, Vol. 15, No. 1, 2019; U.S. Army Special Operations Command, 2017, p. 10.

[17] Frank L Goldstein and Benjamin F. Findley, eds., *Psychological Operations: Principles and Case Studies*, Air University Press, 1996, p. 27–28.

broader strategic objectives in a limited proxy war with a rival state during heightened tensions in strategic competition—either to undermine the morale of proxy forces directly, or to undermine an adversary's willingness to support that proxy.

Economic Effects

The influence pillar of SOF's value proposition for strategic disruption can also help to disrupt adversary efforts by creating time and space for economic assistance and investment to lock in strategic effects in support of U.S. objectives. For example, in 1948, the United States was concerned about the influence of Soviet-supported communist elements in Italy and France. Because of a series of Communist party victories in Europe, "U.S. leaders feared that Western Europe was on the edge of disaster." [18] Elections in Italy in particular "became an apocalyptic test of strength between communism and democracy for the leaders of the U.S. government."[19] As a result of Europe's situation, the U.S. government executed a significant influence campaign in Italy to reduce the likelihood that the Communist party would win elections against the more pro-West Christian Democratic party. Using the reach established by VOA, "President Truman broadcast a warning over Voice of America (VOA) that no economic assistance would be forthcoming if the communists won the election."[20] According to one scholar, "economic assistance and the promise of prosperity became a bludgeon, which the United States held against the Left."[21] VOA successfully pushed narratives that laid bare the economic opportunity cost of embracing Communist influences, thereby disrupting their electoral appeal, and enabling the eventual strategic success of economic integration between Europe and the United States as a tool to contain Soviet expansionism.

---

[18] James E. Miller, "Taking Off the Gloves: The United States and the Italian Elections of 1948," *Diplomatic History*. Vol. 7, No. 1, 1983, p. 35.

[19] Miller, 1983, p. 36.

[20] Larson et al., 2009, p. 138.

[21] Miller, 1983, p. 36.

CHAPTER 7

The Understand Pillar of Strategic Disruption

The understand pillar of SOF's value proposition for strategic disruption entails efforts to extract strategically relevant information from politically sensitive, contested, or denied environments. This concept is encapsulated in the current definition of special reconnaissance, a core SOF activity, which includes "reconnaissance and surveillance actions conducted . . . in hostile, denied, or diplomatically and/or politically sensitive environments to collect or verify information."[1] It also includes broader cultural understanding and relationship-building that occurs as a result of persistent SOF presence and engagement in a given area of operations.

The understand pillar can contribute to strategic disruption by providing senior leaders deep, contextual understanding about denied or semi-permissive environments, thereby enabling the development of refined strategies for campaigning in those environments. Importantly, SOF can help a larger joint force and nonmilitary partners gain an in-depth understanding of adversaries' competitive strategies and priorities through their ability to build and maintain human networks and physical infrastructure in strategic locations.[2] Others have referred to this approach as developing "an intelligence capability to report on how you win" in strategic competition.[3] In these cases, the disruptive effect on an adversary's strategic or operational design is to deny them the ability to shape the environment through preferred strategies by revealing the intent behind their actions or revealing key vulnerabilities to their approach.

Similarly, SOF's value proposition for strategic disruption through understanding can include providing targeting data against strategic targets and facilitating efforts for force protection of other forces (both military and civilian) operating in those environments pursuing their own strategic effects. These efforts disrupt adversary-preferred strategies more indirectly, primarily by enabling nonmilitary partners to deliver their own operational-level effects that set conditions for eventual strategic gains.

---

[1] Joint Publication 3-05, 2014, p. x. During the Cold War, this was referred to as a strategic intelligence collection, target acquisition, and strategic reconnaissance. See Cleveland and Egel, 2020, pp. 23-26.

[2] John Taft, Liz Gormisky, and Joe Mariani, "Special Operations Forces and Great Power Competition: Talent, Technology, and Organizational Change in the New Threat Environment," Deloitte Insights, 2019, p. 10.

[3] Quote is attributed to former Undersecretary of Defense for Intelligence Michael Vickers, as cited in Taft, Gormisky, and Mariani, 2019, p. 10.

These efforts can be done by SOF either unilaterally or working through a partner force on the ground,[4] and complement other types of intelligence by "obtaining specific, well-defined, time-sensitive information of strategic or operational significance."[5] Though governments and even conventional military formations have a wide array of intelligence capabilities, SOF are uniquely capable of operating among local populations in denied or politically sensitive environments. They can therefore provide a critical ability to understand local conditions where other sources of collection are not available or when a detailed understanding of the local population is an essential input into broader efforts to enable military and nonmilitary strategic effects.

Table 7.1 summarizes a set of historical examples in which understand activities enabled strategic disruption. In the sections that follow, we review these historical vignettes to examine how SOF (or SOF-like forces) pursued strategic disruption to enable friendly strategic outcomes across DIME dimensions of national power.

Diplomatic Effects

The understand pillar of SOF's value proposition can support diplomatic objectives through three primary mechanisms. The first is by leveraging persistent access to local populations to provide diplomats with a deep and nuanced local understanding of an operating environment that can be leveraged to frustrate adversary-preferred strategies. In some cases, this can provide policymakers and diplomats the necessary context for influencing key powerbrokers or political players. In other cases, this understanding can provide policymakers and diplomats information that enables them to expose malign behavior by an adversary and therefore increases the diplomatic or political costs a competitor must pay.[6] One clear example of both cases occurred in Bosnia, where SOF's persistent access to local civic actors as part of the Joint Commission Observer mission provided a tool in "maintaining the peace" of the Dayton Accords by understanding—and then influencing—criminal syndicates, bus company presidents, black marketeers, and religious leaders to incentivize adherence to the terms of the peace.[7]

This understanding can also support broader diplomatic engagement by providing a tool for assessing the effectiveness of broader efforts to promote a nation's interests vis-à-vis a competitor in a third country. In Thailand, for example, a decades-long effort by U.S. SOF

---

[4] Tamir Sinai, "Eyes on Target: 'Stay-Behind' Forces During the Cold War," *War in History*, Vol. 28, No. 3, 2021.

[5] Field Manual 3-05.6, *Army Special Operations Forces Aviation Operations*, U.S. Department of the Army, October 2000, p. 2–6.

[6] Hal Brands, "The Dark Art of Political Warfare: A Primer," American Enterprise Institute, February 2020, p. 8.

[7] Cleveland and Egel, 2020, p. 97–103.

TABLE 7.1

Historical Examples of Understand and Strategic Disruption

Dates	Program (Actor)	Target	Intended Disruptive Effect	Outcome
1941–1945	Kempe Tai (Japan)	Allied forces	Provide force protection of conventional forces through intelligence and counterintelligence	D I **M** E
1944–1945	Alamo Scouts (U.S. Army)	Japan	Provide intelligence about Japanese forces to larger Allied units	D I **M** E
1950	Trudy Jackson (USN)	North Korea	Clandestine insertion to collect intelligence in support of a conventional naval operation	D I **M** E
1956–1984	Detachment A (U.S. SOF)	Soviet Union	Establish networks to sabotage civilian infrastructure in Berlin in case of a Soviet invasion of Western Europe	D I **M** **E**
1965–1971	Prairie Fire (U.S. SOF)	Laos	Emplace sensors, conduct reconnaissance of bases and infiltration routes, direct air strikes to deny adversary safe haven	D I **M** E
1966–present	JUSTMAGTHAI program (U.S.)	Thailand	Long-duration mission to build Thai SOF and enable deep understanding in strategically important region	**D** I M E
1967–1971	Salem House (U.S. SOF)	Cambodia	Intelligence collection and verification, emplace mines to deny adversary safe haven	D I **M** E
1987–1989	Operation Earnest Will (USN)	Kuwait-Iran	Disrupt Iranian threats to Kuwaiti oil tankers through real-time intelligence sharing	**D** I **M** **E**
1992	Operation Restore Hope (U.S. SOF)	Somalia	Force protection for civilians providing development and humanitarian assistance	D I M **E**
1995	Operation Joint Endeavor (U.S. SOF)	Bosnia	Force protection for civilians providing development and humanitarian assistance	D I M **E**
1995–1999	Joint Commission Observer (U.S. SOF)	Bosnia	Provide intelligence on local powerbrokers to enable diplomatic and military leadership	**D** I **M** E
1999	Operation Matrix (U.S. SOF)	Serbia	Degrade support for Milošević from patronage network through detailed network mapping of malign actors to support an information campaign	**D** **I** M **E**
2008	Operation Jacque (U.S. SOF)	FARC	U.S.-enabled Colombian operation to free an imprisoned journalist, deny FARC efforts to raise revenue and impose costs	**D** I **M** E
2014	Bosnian Flood Response (U.S. SOF)	Serbia, Russia	Leverage deep understanding of civil actors to promote legitimacy of Bosnian Armed forces as a counterweight to Serbian and Russian influence	**D** **I** M **E**

NOTE: JUSTMAGTHAI = Joint United States Military Advisory Group Thailand; USN = United States Navy. Bold letters indicate that an example pursued friendly diplomatic (D), informational (I), military (M), or economic (E) outcomes.

to build the capacity of Thai SOF has offered a "strategic dividend [by] providing US insight on Thai perspectives on security . . . [and helped] assess how U.S. actions resonate within governmental and population spheres."[8] In the context of strategic disruption, this deep understanding generated by U.S. SOF's historical presence in Thailand has served as a hedge against growing Chinese influence in Thailand,[9] setting favorable conditions for the United States to maintain friendly relations in pursuit of its own objectives as a result.

A second mechanism—which is more indirect—is by providing intelligence in nonpermissive environments to disrupt adversary advances against partner nations, thereby furthering U.S. diplomatic objectives. Operation Earnest Will, a naval operation that was a central component of U.S. diplomatic engagement with Kuwait and containment of the Soviet Union in the late 1980s,[10] offers an example of this mechanism. Naval efforts to defend Kuwaiti oil tankers from Iranian attacks were enabled by a joint special operations task force—which was forward deployed on two mobile barges in the Persian Gulf and provided real-time intelligence on Iranian vessels. The efforts of this task force thereby set favorable conditions for the success of broader U.S. diplomatic efforts to maintain influence with Kuwait in the face of Soviet offers to mediate the conflict instead.[11]

Informational Effects

Understand activities can support informational objectives by providing critical intelligence to guide the implementation of information campaigns that seek to deliver strategic effects.[12] Operation Matrix is one clear example of the strategic potential of SOF understand activities. PSYOPs efforts in Serbia in 1999 leveraged "detailed intelligence work that resulted in [an] influence diagram of Milosevic's power structure" to execute a strategic information campaign that targeted affiliates of former Serbian President Slobodan Milošević with "e-mail, faxes, and cell phones" and airstrikes.[13] By complicating the willingness of Milošević's closest

---

[8] Brian S. Petit, *Breaking Through the Tension: The Operational Art of Special Operations in Phase Zero*, School of Advanced Military Studies, United States Army Command and General Staff College, 2013. For a discussion of the relationship with the JUSTMAGTHAI, see R. Sean Randolph, *The United States and Thailand: Allied Dynamics, 1950–1985*, Institute of East Asian Studies, University of California, Berkeley, 1986. See also J. "Lumpy" Lumbaca, "The U.S.-Thailand ARSOF Relationship," *Special Warfare*, 2012, p. 52–53.

[9] Zachary Abuza, "America Should Be Realistic About its Alliance with Thailand," *War on the Rocks*, January 2, 2020.

[10] Andrew R. Marvin, "Operation Earnest Will—The U.S. Foreign Policy Behind U.S. Naval Operations in the Persian Gulf 1987–89; A Curious Case," *Naval War College Review*, 2020.

[11] David B. Crist, "Joint Special Operations in Support of Earnest Will," *Joint Forces Quarterly*, Autumn/Winter 2001–2002.

[12] Mitchell, 1999.

[13] Julian Tolbert, "Crony Attack: Strategic Attack's Silver Bullet?" School of Advanced Air and Space Studies, November 2006, p. 32; Michael Moran, "Psyops Employed to Sap Iraqi Spirit," *NBC News*, December

political allies to continue lending him their support,[14] this information campaign sought to erode Milošević's broader hold on power—a strategic goal for the United States.

Military Effects

Understand activities also support military objectives in strategic disruption by providing deep insight and intelligence that can frustrate adversary-preferred strategies by directly enabling combat operations in conflict or by supporting preconflict efforts to posture military forces to deter aggression. Though military formations have many intelligence assets, special operations are uniquely capable of operating among local populations in denied environments. They can therefore provide a critical ability to understand local conditions where other sources of collection are not available or when an understanding of the local population is critical to military operations.

The first mechanism for understand activities to enable military strategic disruption is through providing the situational awareness required to guide campaign planning for population-centric and irregular warfare campaigns to frustrate adversary-preferred strategies. The United States' Joint Commission Observer mission in Bosnia supported the U.S. Stabilization Force commander in the late 1990s with an exquisite understanding of local civil society not available through traditional sources of intelligence, as "the intelligence community had a good grasp on the military personalities but not on the civilians who were actually running the country."[15] Similarly, SOF's persistent engagement in Colombia allowed Special Operations Command South to play an essential coordination role in Operation Jacque, a successful hostage rescue operation in Colombia in 2008, resulting in the rescue of multiple U.S. military contractors, Colombian citizens, and a former Colombian presidential candidate from FARC guerrillas.[16] This approach disrupted the ability of the FARC to leverage hostage taking as a tool to raise revenues and impose costs against the United States, setting continued favorable conditions for the United States to continue to militarily support Colombia along its way to an eventual peace deal with the rebels in 2016.

A second mechanism through which understand activities can enable military strategic disruption is by providing military commanders an additional source of enemy-focused intelligence collection to guide planning to conduct strategically important military operations. This was the impetus behind the formation of the Alamo Scouts during World War II, also known as the 6th Army Special Reconnaissance Unit, which provided intelligence on enemy forces and terrain to guide the operational planning of larger military formations

---

2003; Arkin and Windrem, 2001.

[14] Tolbert, 2006.

[15] Charles T. Cleveland, "Command and Control of the Joint Commission Observer Program: U.S. Army Special Forces in Bosnia," United States Army War College, 2001, p. 11.

[16] Cleveland and Egel, 2020, pp. 134-137.

during operations in the Pacific.[17] Operation Trudy Jackson provides a comparable example of this mechanism in a littoral context during the Korean War, in which a U.S. Navy officer conducted clandestine reconnaissance leveraging indigenous forces to support General MacArthur's Inchon landing in 1950.[18] In these cases, SOF-like capabilities for deep understanding disrupted an adversary's preferred approach by revealing sensitive vulnerabilities, thereby enabling more-effective military operations.

A related third mechanism—probably the best-understood component of SOF's understand value proposition—is the ability for SOF-derived understanding to support targeting efforts that frustrate adversary-preferred strategies as part of larger military campaigns. Real-time intelligence developed by SOF has steadily been employed to guide targeting of high-value targets and infrastructure over the last several decades, using both kinetic and nonkinetic means. During the Vietnam War, U.S. special operations teams operated in both Laos (Prairie Fire) and Cambodia (Salem House) to provide intelligence to support targeting by strategic bombers against materiel targets, enemy forces, and key lines of communication to frustrate the ability of the Viet Cong to receive safe haven and external support.[19] U.S. special operations similarly played a critical role in hunting down Saddam Hussein's Scud missiles during Desert Storm, with SOF teams operating inside Iraq against the mobile Scud platforms.[20] Similar to these examples, SOF's broader efforts during Operation Iraqi Freedom to pioneer the Find-Fix-Finish-Exploit-Analyze-Disseminate (F3EAD) targeting cycle also represented a unique way in which understanding can enable strategic disruption. Specifically, SOF elements leveraged intelligence collected from raids against enemy forces to identify new targets for follow-on operations in an iterative cycle.[21] While each of these examples are less directly applicable to campaigning efforts against rival states short of war, they could prove more relevant in the event that such a competition escalates into limited violence or even a broader proxy war.

A final mechanism through which understand capabilities can enable military strategic disruption is their ability to enable force protection for military forces conducting larger operations. During World War II, the Japanese Kempe-Tai—special agents of the Imperial Japanese Army—provided a critical form of force protection for Japanese forces against allied attacks. Specifically, the Kempe-Tai were inserted behind Allied lines to collect information on U.S. and Allied air bases, operating covert radio transmitting stations to "provide warn-

---

[17] Robinson et al., 2018, pp. 10-14.

[18] Anders Westberg, "In Silence Toward the Unknown: Principles of Special Reconnaissance and Surveillance," Naval Postgraduate School, 2016.

[19] U.S. Senate Armed Services Committee, "Bombings in Cambodia," *Hearings, Ninety-Third Congress, First Session*, U.S. Government Publishing Office, 1973, p. 492–494.

[20] William Rosenau, *Special Operations Forces and Elusive Enemy Ground Targets*, RAND Corporation, MR-1408-AF, 2001.

[21] Charles Faint and Michael Harris, "F3EAD: Ops/Intel Fusion 'Feeds' the SOF Targeting Process," *Small Wars Journal*, January 31, 2012.

ings of impending air raids 24 hours in advance" and functioning as a counterintelligence force to detain and interrogate Allied agents.[22] This approach disrupted the Allies' ability to conduct surprise air raids against conventional Japanese forces, setting favorable conditions for Japanese military success.

Economic Effects

Understand activities can support economic strategic disruption by setting favorable conditions for U.S. economic assistance and by guiding or preparing for economic sabotage that aims to deliver strategic effects.

Specific to setting favorable conditions for U.S. economic assistance, SOF capabilities for understanding can help guide the design and implementation of this assistance to effectively frustrate adversary-preferred strategies, thereby helping other instruments of power achieve broader effects through economic statecraft. For example, a SOF-led Civil Military Support Element in Bosnia and Herzegovina (BiH) in 2014 leveraged its deep understanding of BiH's complex ethnic and political dynamics to support partner provision of disaster assistance following devastating flooding, thereby enhancing the "reputation and utility of the Armed Forces of BiH (AFBiH) in the eyes of the population."[23] These efforts to promote the multiethnic Bosnian Armed Forces successfully "countered the destabilizing effect of the Russian response" to the same flooding after Russia deployed a "small, high-risk rescue force" to assist in Serbia which led "many Bosnian Serbs to look toward Russia for help."[24]

Alongside this direct enabling role, the understand pillar can also provide indirect support to economic objectives by functioning as a force protection tool for on-the-ground development implementers, as was the case during Operation Restore Hope in Somalia (in 1992) and Operation Joint Endeavor in Bosnia (in 1995).[25] Efforts to understand potential threats to these development actors sought to deny local adversaries the ability to threaten their work, setting favorable conditions for the success of the development tool of national power.

Sabotage is the other primary mechanism through which understand activities enable economic strategic disruption. This mechanism often relies upon the Criticality, Accessibility, Recouperability, Vulnerability, Effect, and Recognizability (CARVER) methodological approach to target analysis, which was used during the early years of the Cold War to identify

---

[22] Val L. Ruffo, "The Application of Counterintelligence Force Protection Source Operations (CFSO) in the U.S. Pacific Command," U.S. Army Command and General Staff College, 1996, p. 24.

[23] U.S. Army Special Operations Command, 2017, p. 13.

[24] U.S. Army Special Operations Command, 2017, p. 13.

[25] Deborah Kidwell, "Operation RESTORE HOPE (The OSI in Somalia)," U.S. Air Force Office of Special Investigations, July 9, 2020; David W. Becker, "Coming in from the Cold . . . War: Defense Humint Services Support to Military Operations Other Than War," U.S. Army Command and General Staff College, 2000.

vulnerabilities in adversary critical infrastructure.[26] A prominent example of SOF understand activities enabling economic sabotage was the role played by Detachment A, a clandestine U.S. Special Forces unit that operated in Berlin from 1956 to 1990.[27] This unit leveraged its existing placement and access throughout Berlin to develop and refine plans to target railway bridges, power plants, and waterways in the event of a Soviet incursion.[28] While its plans were never executed, Detachment A's efforts provided an asymmetric option to slow the advance of Warsaw Pact armies across Germany through economic means, primarily rendering Berlin's economic infrastructure unusable and unable to support the Soviet war machine in the event of a successful Soviet occupation.[29]

---

[26] James S. Roach, "Joint Special Operations Targeting: An Alternate Scheme," U.S. Army War College, 1989.

[27] Daniel Carter, "Detachment A Recognized for Cold War Efforts in Commemorative Stone Laying Ceremony," United States Army Special Operations Command News Service, January 31, 2014.

[28] James Stejskal, *Special Forces Berlin: Clandestine Cold War Operations of the US Army's Elite, 1956–1990*, Casemate, 2017.

[29] Michael Peck, "This Special Forces Unit Was Trained to Attack Russia from Germany During the Cold War," *The National Interest*, July 2020.

CHAPTER 8

The Target Pillar of Strategic Disruption

The target pillar of SOF's value proposition in strategic disruption includes actions to seize, destroy, disrupt, or secure key personnel, equipment, or infrastructure in politically sensitive, contested, or denied environments.[1] Over the past two decades, the focus of SOF's targeting efforts has primarily been on identifying and neutralizing high-value terrorists in a networked approach.[2] Historically, however, this capability has focused on a broader range of possible targets and activities with clear utility for strategic disruption as part of strategic competition campaigns short of war.

Targeting efforts may contribute to strategic disruption by signaling commitment to an adversary or ally, demonstrating military capabilities and reach into denied areas, or creating outsized psychological effects that degrade an adversary's morale or will to fight.[3] SOF's employment of precision targeting may also support a broader campaign by creating the time and space for diplomatic, military, or other policy options to achieve strategic effects themselves.[4]

Table 8.1 summarizes a set of historical examples in which targeting activities enabled strategic disruption. In the sections that follow, we review these historical vignettes to examine how SOF (or SOF-like forces) pursued strategic disruption to enable friendly strategic outcomes across DIME dimensions of national power.

Diplomatic Effects

Precision targeting rarely achieves decisive, strategic effects in the diplomatic realm on its own. Rather, the target pillar of strategic disruption can help create the time and space for diplomatic options to gain traction, possibly obviating the need for military force. While its

---

[1] This definition is adapted from a variety of sources, including Linda Robinson, Daniel Egel, and Ryan Andrew Brown, *Measuring the Effectiveness of Special Operations*, RAND Corporation, RR-2504-A, 2019; U.S. Army Special Operations Command, 2017, p. 4; Joint Publication 3-05, 2014.

[2] Linda Robinson, "The Future of Special Operations: Beyond Kill and Capture," *Foreign Affairs*, November/December 2012.

[3] Austin Long, "The Limits of Special Operations Forces," *PRISM*, Vol. 6, No. 3, 2016, p. 36.

[4] Robinson, Egel, and Brown, 2019, p. xi.

TABLE 8.1

Historical Examples of Target and Strategic Disruption

Dates	Program (Actor)	Target	Intended Disruptive Effect	Outcome			
1940	Seizure of Fort Eben Emael (Germany)	Allies	Disable defenses to allow German conventional forces to advance into Belgium	D	I	**M**	E
1956–84	Detachment A (U.S. SOF)	USSR	Target civilian infrastructure to render Berlin economically weakened in the case of USSR's invasion	D	I	**M**	**E**
1969	Operation Shock/Green Island Raid (Israel)	Egypt	Destroy Egypt's intelligence and early warning installations to reveal vulnerabilities and hasten conflict's conclusion	**D**	I	**M**	E
1976	Raid on Entebbe Airport, Uganda (Israel)	PLO	Demonstrate the reach of Israeli SOF and dissuade terrorist organizations from taking hostages	**D**	**I**	M	E
2007	Destruction of Al Kibar Nuclear Reactor (Israel)	Syria	Set back Syria's nuclear program; signal resolve and capability to nuclear proliferators in region	**D**	**I**	**M**	E
2010	Sabotage of Iranian Nuclear Program (unknown)	Iran	Set back Iran's nuclear program	**D**	**I**	**M**	E
2011	Bin Laden raid (U.S.)	Al-Qaeda	Degrade adversary command and control; erode ideological appeal	D	**I**	**M**	E
2015	Abu Sayyaf raid (U.S.)	ISIS	Collect key intelligence to enable more-effective targeting by conventional forces	D	I	**M**	E
2021	Colonial Pipeline ransomware attack (Russia)	U.S.	Disrupt U.S. oil and gas distribution at the national level	D	I	M	**E**

NOTE: PLO = Palestine Liberation Organization. Bold letters indicate that an example pursued friendly diplomatic (D), informational (I), military (M), or economic (E) outcomes.

precise origin is not officially known, Stuxnet, a sophisticated malware-based cyber weapon successfully destroyed industrial machinery at the Iranian Natanz uranium enrichment plant, thereby delaying Iran's ability to enrich uranium to weapon-grade levels.[5] Ongoing diplomatic negotiations at the time regarding the future of Iran's nuclear program eventually resulted in the Joint Comprehensive Plan of Action agreement to reduce sanctions on the Iranian economy in exchange for Iran ceasing its pursuit of nuclear weapons.

Precision targeting can also provide policymakers with options to shape the political conditions surrounding ongoing disputes between competing nations—for example, by limiting

---

[5] Ronald L. Lendvay, "Shadows of Stuxnet: Recommendations for U.S. Policy on Critical Infrastructure Cyber Defense Derived from the Stuxnet Attack," Naval Postgraduate School, March 2016.

the scope of a conflict or preventing it from escalating. Israeli raids during the Egyptian-Israel War of Attrition (1969–1970) demonstrated the utility of precision targeting in reducing the potential for military escalation and limiting levels of violence. The use of raids by Israeli SOF were designed "to reduce Egyptian morale, undermine confidence in the regime, and cause Egypt to move additional forces into the rear area and away from the front lines."[6] Equally important, however, was the imperative to limit the scope of the conflict and control the violence to avoid sparking any further Soviet involvement in support of their Egyptian client.[7] This specific diplomatic objective could only be accomplished through the use of precision targeting. And yet, some precision targeting efforts may incur diplomatic and political costs as well. The U.S. raid that killed Osama bin Laden in 2011, as an example, precipitated a broader crisis in U.S.-Pakistani relations over the operation deep inside Pakistani territory.

Information Effects

Targeting also contributes to strategic disruption in the information domain by sowing uncertainty and doubt in the minds of adversary leaders, forces, and populations. SOF's ability to discreetly target an adversary's forces, facilities, and infrastructure can create psychological effects that, for example, interrupt an adversary's strategic or operational design or instill a lack of resolve.[8]

Targeting can aid in degrading adversary will by illustrating SOF's access and capability for action at a time and place of its choosing. Such demonstrations can also bolster allies' will and co-opt neutral states to support shared interests.[9] Israel's covert strike on Syria's al-Kibar nuclear reactor in 2007 neutralized that nation's nuclear program, but its strategic effect in the information domain was primarily to send a message to other actors in the region that Israel was willing and able to use military force to disrupt covert nuclear weapon development in denied areas.[10] Israeli Prime Minister Ehud Olmert outlined this logic at the time, noting that such a strike would "kill two birds with one stone" and "send a message dissuading Iran from pursuing its own nuclear program."[11] Israel's 1969 raid on Green Island—a key

---

[6] W. Andrew Terrill, "The Nature and Value of Commando Operations During the Egyptian-Israeli War of Attrition," *Small Wars and Insurgencies*, Vol. 8, No. 2, 1997, p. 24.

[7] Terrill, 1997, p. 24.

[8] U.S. Army Futures Command, "Army Futures Command Concept for Special Operations 2028," September 18, 2020.

[9] David A. Broyles and Brody Blankenship, *The Role of Special Operations Forces in Global Competition*, Center for Naval Analyses, April 2017, p. 29.

[10] Austin Carson and Keren Yarhi-Milo, "Covert Communication: The Intelligibility and Credibility of Signaling in Secret," *Security Studies*, Vol. 26, No. 1, 2016, p. 133.

[11] David Makovsky, "The Silent Strike: How Israel Bombed a Syrian Nuclear Installation and Kept it Secret," *New Yorker*, September 10, 2012.

component of Egypt's air defense network that had a reputation as being an impenetrable fortress—similarly demonstrated Israel's ability to exploit Egypt's strategic vulnerabilities at a critical point in the War of Attrition.[12] Israel's hostage rescue raid at Entebbe Airport in Uganda "demonstrated the long reach of Israeli SOF,"[13] bolstering deterrence against similar hostage-taking ventures in the future.

Eliminating adversary leadership through targeting may also have a profound effect on the morale of an adversary. Arguably the primary strategic value of the United States' successful raid on Osama bin Laden was not its military impact on Al-Qaeda as an organization but rather the symbolic and psychological effect of the raid, given the almost mythical influence bin Laden had in Salafi jihadist circles and his demonstrated ability to elude capture.[14] The raid also demonstrated to current and potential adversaries the capabilities of U.S. SOF to reach into nonpermissive environments.

Military Effects

The target component of SOF's value proposition for strategic disruption can also enhance the effectiveness of conventional military operations. Specifically, targeting can collect incidental intelligence to drive future military operations, seize key terrain, and conduct other activities that facilitate the introduction of conventional forces or support their maneuver.[15]

SOF targeting efforts can set the conditions required for successful conventional operations that pursue operational and strategic effects. For example, in one of the most prominent direct action missions of World War II, German paratroopers assaulted and captured the Belgian fortress of Eben Emael in 1940, frustrating the Allies' ability to defend key terrain through its prepared defenses and enabling the introduction of conventional forces into Belgium before Allied units could provide reinforcements.[16] Similarly, the Israeli raid on Green Island in 1969 created a gap in Egyptian air defense radar coverage that Israeli aircraft exploited during follow-on operations.[17] Indeed, during the broader War of Attrition, Israel relied heavily upon commando raids to achieve their objectives, often to enable

---

[12] Ahmed S. Khalidi, "The War of Attrition," *Journal of Palestine Studies*, Vol. 3, No. 1, 1973, p. 64. Also see Long, 2016, p. 36.

[13] Long, 2016, p. 37.

[14] Vanda Felbab-Brown, "The Implications of Osama bin Laden's Death for the War in Afghanistan and Global Counterterrorism Efforts," Brookings Institution, May 2, 2011; Jenna Jordan, "Attacking the Leader, Missing the Mark: Why Terrorist Groups Survive Decapitation Strikes," *International Security*, Vol. 34, No. 4, 2014.

[15] U.S. Army Futures Command, 2020, p. 24.

[16] Long, 2016.

[17] Terrill, 1997, p. 16.

effects from conventional airpower.[18] In these two cases, synchronizing special and conventional operations allowed the decisive tactical success gained from targeting to have a decisive operational-to-strategic military effects as well.[19]

Targeting may also set the conditions for follow-on disruption operations against priority targets by collecting key information or intelligence. For example, the U.S. SOF raid on the Islamic State's oil minister Abu Sayyaf in 2015 captured troves of documents that shed new light on how the terrorist organization generated revenue. Prior to the capture of this information, the U.S. government struggled to degrade the Islamic State's resource base because most of the group's revenue was internally derived from oil sales and tax revenue. The intelligence from the SOF raid was critical in helping the U.S. Air Force develop the high-impact targets in the oil supply chain that would have the greatest impact on degrading the group's oil enterprise.[20]

While many of these historical examples focus on armed conflict, SOF's targeting value proposition for strategic disruption can serve two purposes in competition as well. First, SOF's ability to reach deep into denied environments for sabotage purposes against an adversary's key infrastructure or points of vulnerability serves a deterrent purpose short of war, potentially forcing adversaries to expend resources protecting critical internal lines of communication. Second, SOF's targeting value proposition can help support key allies and partners to resolve internal security threats, potentially disrupting efforts by strategic competitors to foment internal instability in U.S. allies and partners or degrade U.S. influence by demonstrating the inability of the United States to defend a partner from adversary coercion.

Economic Effects

Targeting can also enable strategic disruption by degrading an adversary's economic resource base, disrupting supply chains, damaging industrial protection facilities, or committing other acts of sabotage that physically damage a military or government's ability to function.

As an example of targeting efforts to disrupt supply chains, a cyberattack on Colonial Pipelines in 2021 enabled Russia-linked cybercrime group DarkSide to temporarily disable the largest fuel pipeline in the United States for six days. The disruption caused gas stations to go without fuel and induced panic buying that caused the price of gas to spike in certain mar-

---

[18] Terrill, 1997, p. 25.

[19] William McRaven, *Spec Ops: Case Studies in Operational Warfare: Theory and Practice*, Presidio Press, 1996, Chapter 2.

[20] Becca Wasser, Stacie L. Pettyjohn, Jeffrey Martini, Alexandra T. Evans, Karl P. Mueller, Nathaniel Edenfield, Gabrielle Tarini, Ryan Haberman, and Jalen Zeman, *The Air War Against the Islamic State: The Role of Airpower in Operation Inherent Resolve*, RAND Corporation, RR-A388-1, 2021, pp. 207–208; Adam Szubin, "Remarks of Acting Under Secretary Adam Szubin on Countering the Financing of Terrorism at the Paul H. Nitze School of Advanced International Studies," press release, U.S. Department of the Treasury, October 10, 2016.

kets across the United States.[21] By comparison, the NotPetya cyberattack that hit the global shipping company Maersk in 2017 cost the company between $200 million and $300 million and briefly shut down the Port of Los Angeles' largest cargo terminal, illustrating the massive economic impact that targeting of supply chains can have.[22] These activities had the primary goal of fomenting social instability through disruption in the economic domain.

During the Cold War, U.S. SOF in Berlin (Detachment A) also planned to target railway bridges, power plants, and waterways to sabotage this infrastructure in the event of Soviet occupation.[23] Allied SOF in World War II executed similar economic sabotage, targeting "rail lines of communication, hydroelectric power production and distribution facilities, telecommunications facilities, canal locks, port facilities, factories engaged in the manufacture of war materiel, and military supply dumps or other targets."[24]

---

[21] Tsvetan Tsvetanov and Srishti Slaria, "The Effect of the Colonial Pipeline Shutdown on Gasoline Prices," *Economics Letters,* No. 209, December 2021.

[22] Andy Greenberg, "The Untold Story of NotPetya, the Most Devastating Cyberattack in History," WIRED, August 22, 2018.

[23] Peck, 2020.

[24] Votel et al., 2016, p. 104.

CHAPTER 9

Future Strategic Disruption in Cyberspace

Cyberspace operations (cyber) and electromagnetic spectrum operations (EMSO) are projected to have an increasingly important role in competition with near-peer adversaries. Cyber will be used in crisis and conflict both to collect intelligence and to influence adversary systems.[1] Superiority in the electromagnetic spectrum "brings important advantages to any cost imposition strategy," with EMSO providing DoD the ability to "protect expensive friendly capabilities from disruption or attrition, while simultaneously denying or degrading the effectiveness of adversaries' high-priced systems."[2]

While we included some instances of cyber or electromagnetic spectrum–based strategic disruption in our prior analyses of each pillar of strategic disruption, our goal in this chapter is to explore how future trends in these capabilities are likely to drive changes in SOF's tactical and operational ability to execute strategic disruption campaigns—and not how these capabilities are uniquely able to deliver DIME-specific effects. We explored cyber and EMSO capabilities in this way for two main reasons. One, the rate of technological change in the cyber and EMSO space is rapid and accelerating, particularly when compared with other tactical capabilities employed by military forces. Second, perhaps as a result, leaders across the special operations community have signaled the need for greater integration between SOF and cyber capabilities.[3] As a result, it is worth exploring how developments in these capabilities are likely to affect SOF's ability to execute strategic disruption campaigns in the future.

Cyber and EMSO are two distinct capabilities.[4] However, this chapter examines them collectively as they relate to SOF's future potential for strategic disruption in two ways, to the extent that cyber and EMSO can both enable and be enabled by special operations activities. Defensive cyber and EMSO capabilities are likely to prove critical in the survivability of SOF tactical units executing strategic disruption activities, particularly in nonpermissive environ-

---

[1] DoD, *Summary of the Department of Defense Cyber Strategy*, 2018a.

[2] DoD, *Electromagnetic Spectrum Superiority Strategy*, October 2020b, p. 5.

[3] See, for example, Todd C. Lopez, "Parent Services Integration a Top Priority for Special Operations Components," Department of Defense News, May 2, 2022.

[4] The Army discusses these capabilities in a single doctrinal publication: Field Manual 3-12, *Cyberspace and Electronic Warfare Operations*, U.S. Department of the Army, August 2021.

ments.[5] And offensive cyber and EMSO capabilities are likely to present new vectors through which SOF can achieve strategic disruption, both by creating space for SOF tactical units to operate and through SOF units providing physical access to enable use of these capabilities.[6]

Table 9.1 summarizes the synergies between these capabilities and our five pillars of SOF's value proposition for strategic disruption. The remainder of this chapter examines cyber and EMSO's role in strategic disruption across each pillar in greater detail, exploring the relevance of both defensive and offensive capabilities in this space.

Cyber and EMSO and the Resist Pillar

There are at least four mechanisms through which cyber and EMSO can enable SOF's resist pillar for strategic disruption, which involves support to foreign security forces or groups within a foreign population by an external power to coerce, disrupt, or overthrow an adversary government or occupying power. First, cyber and EMSO can create the time and space necessary for SOF and SOF-like forces to execute broader resistance or UW operations. Russian actions in Ukraine prior to its invasion of Crimea and support to rebel groups in the Donbas in 2014 provide a vivid illustration of this approach. Specifically, Russia "disconnected, jammed, and attacked digital, telephone, and cyber communications throughout Ukraine" and "enlisted virtual 'privateers' and bounty hunters to conduct cyberattacks

TABLE 9.1

Cyber and EMSO Synergies with SOF Pillars of Strategic Disruption

Pillars	Synergies with Cyber and EMSO Capabilities
Resist	Enable or support a resistance movement or insurgency by manipulating, denying, disrupting, degrading, or destroying information systems, devices, and networks that belong to a government or occupying power
Support	Bolster information capabilities of a host nation to protect against subversion, lawlessness, insurgency, terrorism, and other threats to their internal security, stability, and legitimacy
Influence	Provide a platform for disseminating information or influence specific audiences through targeted disruption
Understand	Provide new mechanisms for data collection; enable cyberspace superiority
Target	Provide proximity to systems for exploitation; leverage cyber/EMSO to create opportunities for other targeting

---

[5] Patrick Tucker, "Army SOF Units Are Getting Smaller, More Self-Reliant as Focus Shifts to China, Russia," *Defense One*, May 20, 2021; Ethan Brown, "After Afghanistan, U.S. Forces Are Ill-Prepared for Electronic Warfare Elsewhere," *The Hill*, December 7, 2021.

[6] Mark Pomerlau, "Army Special Forces Want to Integrate More with Other Military Units on Info Warfare," C4ISRNet, August 19, 2021.

against Ukrainian government information and logistics infrastructure."[7] This "choreo-graphed cyber disinformation and cyberattack bought time and space for laptop-carrying Spetsnaz to conduct unconventional warfare" in the Donbas region thereafter.[8]

Second, cyber and EMSO can be used to harden resistance forces, enhancing the efficacy and influence of these forces as insurgent actors contesting the legitimacy of an occupying or established power.[9] This reflects the reality that cyberspace capabilities "provide resistance movements with great reach in their external and international communications and a wide range of internal communications options," although they also present many opportunities for state authorities to compromise these mechanisms of communication.[10]

Third, cyber may provide a mechanism for SOF to conduct activities in this pillar without deploying forces physically into denied areas, potentially reducing cost and risk and allowing for scalability.[11] A capability for remote advise and assist of this nature this does not currently exist in the U.S. military, at least at scale.[12] However, nonstate actors like Al-Qaeda and the Islamic State have used cyber capabilities to recruit, train, and coordinate operations, demonstrating the potential potency of such approaches.[13]

Fourth, cyber capabilities may provide a new type of partner force to enable resistance operations—groups with primarily cyber expertise—that could be mobilized by SOF to resist a government or occupying power. There are a wide variety of partisan forces focused on cyber operations currently operating across the globe, sometimes described under the moniker of hacktivists. This includes Ukraine's "IT Army," which reportedly includes nearly a half-million Ukrainian civilians engaged in volunteer cyber operations against Russia,[14] a Belarusian group known as the Cyber Partisans,[15] and others. These forces represent new

---

[7] Patrick Michael Duggan, "Strategic Development of Special Warfare in Cyberspace," *Joint Forces Quarterly*, No. 79, October 1, 2015, p. 47.

[8] Duggan, 2015, p. 47.

[9] Kristen Ryan, ed., *Resistance and the Cyber Domain*, United States Army Special Operations Command and Johns Hopkins University Applied Physics Laboratory, 2019.

[10] Ryan, 2019, p. 90.

[11] Ryan S. Gladding and Sean P. McQuade, "Cyber-Enabled Unconventional Warfare: The Convergence of Cyberspace, Social Mobilization, and Special Warfare," Naval Postgraduate School, December 2015; Nicholas A. Bredenkamp and Mark Grzegorzewski, "Supporting Resistance Movements in Cyberspace," *Special Operations Journal*, Vol. 7, No. 1, April 2021, p. 17–28; Sean W. Pascoli and Mark Grzegorzewski, "Technology Adoption in Unconventional Warfare," *The Cyber Defense Review*, 2021.

[12] Gladding and McQuade, 2015.

[13] Gladding and McQuade, 2015.

[14] Sam Schechner, "Ukraine's 'IT Army' Has Hundreds of Thousands of Hackers, Kyiv Says," *Wall Street Journal*, March 4, 2022.

[15] Max Smeets and Brita Achberger, "Cyber Hacktivists Are Busy Undermining Putin's Invasion," *Washington Post*, May 13, 2022.

opportunities for SOF to enable resistance beyond the provision of military support to guerrilla forces.

Cyber and EMSO and the Support Pillar

SOF's support pillar for strategic disruption focuses on the development and preparation of host nation forces' capability and capacity to work alongside or in place of U.S. forces to counter hostile adversary actions. Defensive cyber can enable activities in this pillar by protecting SOF's partner forces, typically through training forces on the basics of defensive cyber, including secure telecommunications and cyber hygiene.[16] This *cybersecurity assistance*—which is used to "secure and operate computer networks, enhance OPSEC [operational security], and enable trusted communications within their forces and between U.S. and supported foreign forces"[17]—is seen as a critical function in helping "partners protect their critical infrastructure or enhance their resilience against information warfare" in competition with China and Russia.[18]

Cybersecurity assistance has reportedly become "one of the most frequently requested" types of support for the National Guard's State Sponsorship Program.[19] Building cyber resilience among foreign partners is also one of the core mandates for the Department of State's Global Engagement Center, whose Network Engagement and Training Cell coordinates efforts to "establish, train, connect, mobilize, and maintain active networks of foreign civil society influencers and government communicators."[20] Comparable support to partner elements could be provided by the special forces communications sergeant on an Army Operational Detachment-Alpha, who could work to protect partner forces and create opportunities for SOF or other U.S. elements to exploit adversary vulnerabilities.[21]

---

[16] Whitney Kassel and Philip Reiner, "'Cyber FID': The Role of Cyber in Foreign Internal Defense," in Zachary S. Davis, Frank Gac, Christopher Rager, Philip Reiner, and Jennifer Snow, eds., *Strategic Latency Unleashed: The Role of Technology in a Revisionist Global Order and the Implications for Special Operations Forces*, Lawrence Livermore National Laboratory, 2021.

[17] Joint Publication 3-22, *Foreign Internal Defense*, U.S. Department of Defense, February 2, 2021, p. I–19.

[18] Quote is attributed to Senator Gary Peters in U.S. Senate Armed Services Committee, "To Receive Testimony on United States Special Operations Command and United States Cyber Command in Review of the Defense Authorization Request for Fiscal Year 2022 and the Future Years Defense Program," hearing transcript, March 25, 2021.

[19] Quote is attributed to General Daniel Hokanson in Lauren C. Williams, "Cyber Assistance Ranks High on National Guard Requested Services, Chief Says," *FCW*, May 10, 2022.

[20] U.S. Department of State, "Global Engagement Center (R/GEC)," undated.

[21] Kassel and Reiner, 2021, p. 374.

Cyber and EMSO and the Influence Pillar

The influence pillar of SOF strategic disruption involves informing and shaping the attitudes, behavior, and decisions of foreign actors in support of U.S. interests. There are two primary mechanisms through which cyber and EMSO can enable SOF activities in the influence pillar. The primary mechanism is through additional technical means of presenting themes and narratives to target audiences, either broadcast broadly to a wide audience or targeted selectively to select individuals or population groups.[22] Indeed, one study concludes that "controlling cyberspace (and the intersecting electromagnetic spectrum) could eventually be tantamount to controlling the information environment."[23]

The second mechanism—which has been described as "Influence Cyber Operations"—is a range of "more intrusive ways to influence specific audiences . . . [using tools that] change, compromise, inject, destroy, or steal information by accessing information systems and networks."[24] The Russian-orchestrated cyberattacks against Estonia in 2007 offer an example of this mechanism, with a coordinated distributed denial of service attack affecting the ability of the Estonian government and critical economic sectors to govern as a punishment for an ongoing dispute with Russia over the status of Soviet war memorials in Tallinn.[25]

Cyber and EMSO and the Understand Pillar

SOF's understand pillar of strategic disruption entails efforts to extract strategically relevant information from semi-permissive or denied environments. Cyber can enable SOF operations in this pillar by providing an added mechanism through which SOF can gain insights into local populations, adversary capabilities, and even requirements for training local partner forces.[26] Deep understanding of a given operational environment, a core element of this pillar, is also likely to enable the employment of cyber and EMSO capabilities by other military forces for strategic disruption purposes. Thus, while tactical cyber capabilities are likely to prove critical to the survivability of special reconnaissance elements seeking to gain under-

---

[22] Joint Publication 3-12, *Cyberspace Operations*, U.S. Department of Defense, June 8, 2018, p. I-7.

[23] Isaac R. Porche III, Christopher Paul, Michael York, Chad C. Serena, Jerry M. Sollinger, Elliot Axelband, Endy Y. Min, Bruce J. Held, *Redefining Information Warfare Boundaries for an Army in a Wireless World*, RAND Corporation, MG-113-A, 2013, p. xvii.

[24] Pascal Brangetto and Matthijs A. Veenendaal, "Influence Cyber Operations: The Use of Cyberattacks in Support of Influence Operations," paper presented at the 8th International Conference on Cyber Conflict, 2016, p. 113.

[25] Rain Ottis, "Analysis of the 2007 Cyber Attacks Against Estonia from the Information Warfare Perspective," proceedings of the 7th European Conference on Information Warfare and Security, Cooperative Cyber Defence Centre of Excellence, 2008.

[26] For a discussion, see Stavros Atlamazoglou, "The U.S. Is Scrambling to Deal with Cyberattacks, and That May Mean New Roles and Missions for Special-Ops Units," *Business Insider*, June 10, 2021.

standing for strategic disruption purposes, this same understanding will also be critical for efforts to gain cyberspace superiority by other elements of the joint force.[27]

Cyber and EMSO and the Target Pillar

SOF's target pillar of strategic disruption includes actions to seize, destroy, or disrupt enemy personnel, equipment, infrastructure, or operations in politically sensitive, contested, or denied environments. Cyber and EMSO capabilities both enable and are enabled by this pillar of SOF strategic disruption. These capabilities can enable SOF targeting by providing additional means of gaining physical access to key infrastructure or locations for targeting purposes.[28] These capabilities are also enabled by SOF strategic disruption through targeting. The most prominent example of this would be through ground forces providing physical access to an electronic system. In some cases, this could be done remotely, with a SOF element setting up a position in proximity to a targeted system. In other circumstances, particularly given efforts to harden computer and electronic systems against remote infiltration, offensive cyber and EMSO operations "might require a human asset to perform physical tasks, such as connecting an alligator clip, splicing a wire, or inserting a thumb drive . . . [w]hen a human asset is required, there can be no substitute."[29]

---

[27] U.S. Department of the Air Force, "Special Reconnaissance," webpage, undated.

[28] Pomerlau, 2021.

[29] Quote is from Isaac R. Porche III, Christopher Paul, Chad C. Serena, Colin P. Clarke, Erin-Elizabeth Johnson, and Drew Herrick, *Tactical Cyber: Building a Strategy for Cyber Support to Corps and Below*, RAND Corporation, RR-1600-A, 2017, p. 51. The ellipsis in this quote corresponds to a paragraph break in the original text, though the sentences are adjacent. See also Jonas van Hooren, "The Imperative Symbiotic Relationship Between SOF and Cyber: How Dutch Special Operation Forces Can Support Cyber Operations," Naval Postgraduate School, 2019, p. 86, 92.

CHAPTER 10

Findings and Implications for Future SOF

This chapter concludes our analysis by discussing key findings from our analysis of historical strategic disruption by SOF and SOF-like forces, as well as implications of our broader concept for strategic disruption for future SOF defense policymakers in campaigning and strategic competition.

We begin by summarizing the various mechanisms through which SOF-led strategic disruption can set favorable conditions for strategic outcomes across the DIME spectrum, as identified in our historical analysis in the preceding chapters. We then summarize relevant insights from this analysis across the three core tenets of strategic disruption diagnosed at the beginning of the report—its proactive nature, its focus on frustrating adversary-preferred strategies, and its ability to enable effects across the DIME spectrum. We conclude by diagnosing the implications of these findings for future SOF and defense policymakers in strategic competition. A separate, companion report also applies this framework for strategic disruption to a detailed playbook of potential Chinese People's Liberation Army missions, tasks, and vulnerabilities in both peacetime competition and in the event of a low-intensity conflict between China and the United States.[1]

Mechanisms for SOF-Led Strategic Disruption Across the DIME

Across our various historical examples of strategic disruption, we identified a series of mechanisms through which SOF (and SOF-like forces) can frustrate adversary-preferred strategies to enable strategic disruption across the DIME spectrum. These mechanisms are summarized in Table 10.1, organized by each pillar of SOF capability.

In terms of setting favorable conditions for the achievement of diplomatic strategic goals, we found frequent instances in which SOF sought to deliver physical or cognitive effects to frustrate an adversary's efforts that ultimately enhanced the likelihood for success of a diplomatic agreement, enforced adherence to a diplomatic agreement, or simply shaped the policy

---

[1] Timothy R. Heath, Eric Robinson, Christian Curriden, Derek Grossman, Sale Lilly, Daniel Egel, and Gabrielle Tarini, *Disrupting the Chinese Military in Competition and Low-Intensity Conflict: An Analysis of People's Liberation Army Missions, Tasks, and Potential Vulnerabilities*, RAND Corporation, 2023.

TABLE 10.1

Mechanisms for SOF-Led Strategic Disruption to Enable Strategic Effects

SOF Capability	Diplomatic Competition	Informational Competition	Military Competition	Economic Competition
Resist	• Incentivize a change in adversary policy • Shape resistance movements	• Undermine adversary legitimacy	• Fix adversary conventional forces • Deter adversary aggression through resistance	• Extend an adversary to commit resources • Disrupt or sabotage critical infrastructure
Support	• Incentivize diplomatic settlements • Shape partner's policy preferences	• Expand influence in contested areas • Deny adversary objectives through resilience	• Promote benefits of military-to-military relations • Deny adversary objectives through internal stability	• Buy time for long-term economic assistance
Influence	• Undermine adversary legitimacy • Enhance support for diplomacy	• Disrupt adversary narratives through strategic messaging	• Deceive adversary understanding of friendly strength • Undermine adversary morale	• Buy time for long-term economic assistance
Understand	• Expand diplomatic engagement with local populations • Share strategic intelligence with partners	• Inform population-centric messaging campaigns	• Support operations in population-centric campaigns • Enable conventional operations • Enable targeting	• Inform economic/ humanitarian assistance • Identify economic vulnerabilities to sabotage
Target	• Incentivize a diplomatic settlement • Control escalation through limited use of force	• Generate adversary uncertainty over operational reach • Degrade adversary morale and will	• Target critical infrastructure • Generate iterative, network disruption	• Degrade adversary resources base through sabotage

SOURCE: RAND Arroyo Center analysis based upon historical examples of U.S., partner, and adversary examples of SOF and SOF-like forces attempting strategic disruption of adversary objectives.

preferences of an adversary or partner nation in line with friendly political interests. In these cases, SOF's primary potential in enabling diplomatic outcomes through strategic disruption came from its ability to reach into politically sensitive or denied areas.

Regarding strategic disruption to enable informational competition, we found frequent instances of SOF leveraging various capabilities—not just for influence—to execute offensive efforts to undermine an adversary's informational objectives, including efforts to degrade their morale or will to fight or undermine their legitimacy over relevant populations. We also saw more defensive mechanisms for strategic disruption in the informational domain focused on insulating friendly populations from adversary malign influence or weakening the efficacy of an adversary's narratives through counter messaging. In these cases, SOF's primary potential in enabling informational outcomes through strategic disruption came from its deep understanding of local populations and ability to work closely with partner forces.

In terms of setting favorable conditions for military success in competition, we identified various mechanisms through which SOF and SOF-like forces sought to create strategic military gains largely as a direct result of their own campaigns, often through resistance and targeting efforts to asymmetrically shape an adversary's willingness to employ military aggression. These cases were few, however, in comparison with more-frequent instances in which SOF sought to frustrate adversary-preferred strategies by enabling broader military success by other actors—including by promoting the benefits of a military relationship with the United States as a counterweight to rival influence, shaping an adversary's response to follow-on operations by other conventional forces, undermining or deceiving an adversary's military forces, or enabling deep understanding of a broader area of operations in which military operations are ongoing. While many of these mechanisms were drawn from historical examples of SOF activities in conflict, many apply to SOF's role in establishing preconflict deterrence or potentially SOF's role supporting a partner dealing with an internal threat backed by an external rival state. Either way, SOF's primary potential in enabling military outcomes through strategic disruption was in its ability to employ specialized capabilities that delivered outsized or asymmetric disruptive effects relative to the level of investment required.

Finally, the primary mechanisms through which SOF sought to enable economic competition included efforts to buy time and space for long-term economic assistance, as well as more-direct efforts to extend an adversary's resources or disrupt their critical infrastructure in a more intensified, likely limited conflict. Compared with the other components of the DIME spectrum, these mechanisms suggest a more limited role for SOF in strategic disruption that enables economic strategic objectives. And yet, SOF's primary potential in this space may be in its ability to maintain a long-duration approach that frustrates adversary efforts to destabilize conditions in which long-term economic assistance from the United States can lock in friendly strategic objectives.

Key Findings and Takeaways

To better understand the implications of these mechanisms for strategic disruption on future SOF, we summarize key findings from this historical analysis related to each of the three underlying tenets of strategic disruption identified in the early chapters—the need to be proactive, the need to frustrate adversary-preferred strategies, and the need to enable multiple instruments of national power.

The Strategic Potential of Being Proactive

At the start of this report, we noted that being proactive in strategic disruption entailed the deliberate use of military forces to set conditions that are favorable for the achievement of friendly strategic objectives. This framing seeks to break the United States of its often-reactive approach to competitors' efforts to win without fighting, in that America's conventional warfighting strength often means that competitors will tailor their acts of coercion short of war to make a conventional military response by the United States appear risky or even disproportional in response.

Across our historical examples of strategic disruption, we saw how proactive campaigns can enable broader strategic effects in two different ways. First, we found that proactive attempts at strategic disruption can enable direct and immediate strategic outcomes, often in a time-bound manner, to clear a specific hurdle to the success of some friendly strategic objective. Success for these strategic disruption campaigns is often measured in terms of whether an adversary is prevented from achieving a specific intermediate objective, measurable against clear criteria. Examples include VOA's role in conditioning potential economic support to Italy on the outcome of Italian elections in 1948, as well as U.S. SOF's role in promoting adherence to diplomatic agreements during the Joint Commission Observer mission in Bosnia and even Russian SOF and PMC support to prevent the defeat of Assad Regime military forces during the Syrian Civil War. In each of these cases (and others identified throughout the report), SOF or SOF-like forces conducted deliberate operations to achieve discrete objectives, often bounded in time against clear measurable conditions.

And yet, we found that proactive attempts at strategic disruption can also enable indirect and delayed strategic outcomes, shaping broader conditions in which strategic competition and potential conflict is likely to occur over longer durations to enable strategic success. While our case study approach did not allow us to say definitively whether such indirect campaigns are more frequent than direct and immediate campaigns, most of the mechanisms for strategic disruption identified as a result of our analysis (Table 10.1) enable strategic outcomes over the long run. These campaigns are still proactive, in that they involve getting out ahead of an adversary's strategic or operational design and not just responding to their advances. And yet, such campaigns will often focus on slowly eroding an adversary's capacity or will to achieve their own objectives through a preferred course of action, primarily to create space and opportunity for other instruments of national power to achieve their own long-term objectives. As a result, success in these campaigns is often more difficult to measure or predict in advance. This does not mean such campaigns are less likely to succeed, although we did not attempt a comparative analysis of the effectiveness of such campaigns in this report.

Examples of more-indirect and delayed strategic disruption campaigns include the CIA's Cold War support to Tibetan resistance that later enabled a broader diplomatic split between the USSR and China, U.S. SOF support to Colombian security forces that facilitated long-term economic development under Plan Colombia, and U.S. SOF support to Thai SOF under the JUSTMAGTHAI construct that enabled a deepening of the U.S.-Thai bilateral relationship in multiple domains over time. In each of these cases (and others identified throughout the report), the role of SOF and SOF-like forces was primarily to set conditions that widened the aperture of potential opportunities for strategic success in future years.

The Strategic Potential of Frustrating Adversary-Preferred Strategies

The second tenet of strategic disruption is that it seeks to frustrate adversary-preferred strategies. Specifically, we assessed that strategic disruption entails deliberate efforts to delay, degrade, or deny an adversary's ability to achieve core interests via their own preferred courses of action. This framing seeks to expand upon growing discussion of the military's role in imposing costs, creating dilemmas, and targeting the vulnerabilities of rival states short of war. While these terms are useful in their simplicity, they are insufficient on their own to explain how costs can be imposed, dilemmas created, and vulnerabilities targeted to generate positive strategic outcomes for the United States and not just unintended escalation in response.

This research revealed a number of insights into how frustrating an adversary's strategic design can yield friendly strategic gains. First, we found that efforts to frustrate adversary-preferred strategies often enable strategic success by incentivizing an adversary to embrace suboptimal approaches. A clear example of this logic is found in Russia's intervention in 2015 to support Assad regime military forces during the Syrian Civil War. Russian SOF, PMC, and airpower successfully stemmed the tide of a potential military victory by anti-Assad forces (their preferred approach), leaving most efforts to constrain the Assad regime primarily to the diplomatic realm where they were less likely to succeed. Moreover, such diplomatic engagement only strengthened Russia's reputation as an essential diplomatic powerbroker in the region (its core strategic priority for intervention). We saw similar logic in the United States' efforts to support El Salvador's internal struggle against Soviet-backed insurgents in the 1980s.

Second, we found that efforts to frustrate adversary-preferred strategies, rather than simply deter by punishment or via cost imposition, can help manage escalation. Strategic disruption's focus on frustrating an adversary's decision space often leaves the adversary decision with some room to still pursue their own objectives albeit through alternative approaches. This approach to shaping adversary behavior is more nuanced than a straight cost imposition approach, which seeks to deter by direct punishment and could incur a similar punishment in response.[2] Across our historical examples, we saw multiple instances of efforts to frustrate adversary strategies being used to manage or limit escalation in this manner. This includes Israeli SOF raids during the Egyptian-Israel War of Attrition to fix Egyptian conventional forces in rear areas, reducing the potential for greater direct confrontation between conventional forces, and reducing incentives for further Soviet intervention in the conflict. On a smaller scale, U.S. SOF efforts under Operation Observant Compass to induce defections from the LRA leveraged information operations to force the group's fighters to dissipate,

---

[2] Michael J. Mazarr, *Understanding Deterrence*, RAND Corporation, PE-295-RC, 2018, p. 2.

thereby obviating the need for a more destructive or costly military campaign to achieve similar effects.

Finally, we found that efforts to frustrate adversary-preferred strategies do not need to be strategic in and of themselves to enable strategic disruption. There are, of course, cases where SOF's disruptive effects approached the strategic level, often in the military domain. This primarily includes efforts to leverage resistance forces and partner nation security forces as an asymmetric deterrent to aggression or to take and hold territory through partner forces. These effects are strategic, in part, because they mostly eliminate the need for a more costly and expansive deployment of conventional forces to achieve similar objectives.

However, the bulk of historical examples of strategic disruption identified in this study began with deliberate acts or campaigns to frustrate adversary-preferred strategies that deliver more tactical and operational disruptions of adversary approaches. U.S. SOF's role in Operation Earnest Will in Kuwait in the late 1980s, for example, focused on providing tactical-level intelligence to Kuwait to disrupt Iranian naval aggression, but its strategic effect was in cementing U.S. influence in Kuwait as a counterweight to Soviet expansionism in the region. Similarly, the CIA's support to the Polish Solidarity Movement under QRHELPFUL had the immediate, more-modest effect of degrading the ability of the Soviet Union to suppress Solidarity's influence within Poland. Strategically, however, this set conditions in which Solidarity could help lead Poland's transition out of communism as part of the broader dissolution of the Soviet Union, a strategic objective for the United States.

The Strategic Potential of Enabling Multiple Instruments of National Power

The final tenet of our concept for strategic disruption is that it sets favorable conditions for multiple instruments of national power to achieve strategic objectives across the DIME spectrum. Specifically, we assessed that efforts to frustrate adversary-preferred strategies through strategic disruption can create the time, space, and opportunities for various instruments of national power to achieve strategic outcomes themselves.

Two specific considerations are worth highlighting. First, we found that disruptive effects on adversary-preferred strategies in one domain can often create the time, space, and opportunities for strategic success in another domain. Across numerous instances in our historical analysis, we saw disruptive effects on an adversary's preferred strategy in one domain ultimately enable friendly strategic objectives in another. Most frequent were instances in which SOF disrupted an adversary's military strategic or operational design, thereby generating diplomatic, influence, or even economic strategic success. For U.S. SOF specifically, this includes efforts to build the capacity of various partner forces to achieve discrete military objectives, including the Philippine Armed Forces, the Iraqi CTS, Colombian security forces, and Thai SOF (under JUSTMAGTHAI)—each of which enabled broader diplomatic, informational, and even economic objectives for the United States and its partners. More creative were instances in which SOF levied or threatened informational, economic, or diplomatic costs upon an adversary as a means of enabling broader military success, including efforts in Bosnia and Serbia to illuminate corruption, shape the behavior of local powerbrokers, and even provide disaster relief as means of decreasing the probability of renewed ethnic conflict. Another example is Detachment A's Cold War mission in Berlin, although never executed, which prepared sabotage options to influence economic pain upon Soviet forces in the event of their occupation of Berlin as a means of slowing their military advance further into NATO territory.

Second, we found that not all strategic opportunities created by strategic disruption campaigns across the DIME spectrum were known in advance of the initial deliberate employment of forces, and that such opportunities often materialized in the course of executing disruption campaigns. This primarily applies to the long duration and delayed types of strategic disruption campaigns identified earlier in this chapter. The CIA's support to Tibetan resistance is the best example of this lesson, in that its paramilitary support to resistance fighters over roughly 15 years eventually provided a bargaining chip for the United States to deepen the growing Sino-Soviet rupture in the 1970s—an opportunity that was not the original goal of the program at its onset in the 1950s. Similarly, U.S. support to the Afghan mujahideen in the 1980s was initially focused on narrower goals of simply extending the Soviets—that is, until the success of these resistance fighters enabled the United States to pursue broader strategic objectives of forcing a complete Soviet withdrawal and degradation in Soviet power projection capabilities.

Of note, this is not to suggest that SOF cannot engage in more-direct and more-immediate strategic disruption campaigns, often in a time-bound manner, to clear a specific hurdle to the success of some friendly strategic objective. It does, however, suggest that strategic disruption could serve as a hedge against future risk in situations in which an adversary's ultimate objectives or preferred approach to achieving their own core interests are likely to develop or change in unknown ways.

Implications for Future SOF

Overall, this research provides concrete examples of the unique potential of SOF to frustrate adversary competitive strategies, particularly in situations in which conventional deterrence alone is an insufficient tool to achieve similar effects. Absent such a capability, the United States military is left to choose between ill-suited escalatory responses as its only recourse to adversary approaches that deliberately seek to avoid high-end conflict.

For the special operations community, this research also provides a clear rubric to motivate future concepts, plans, and analyses that look to harness SOF's unique potential to execute disruptive campaigns that challenge nation-state competitors' efforts to win without fighting. Several implications emerge, summarized below.

Success in strategic disruption should be measured by whether such campaigns are initially able to frustrate adversary-preferred strategies. In our conceptual model for strategic disruption, a deliberate military campaign seeks first to frustrate adversary-preferred strategies as an intermediate outcome, thereby setting favorable conditions for the achievement of a strategic objective in the end. Specifically, our analysis implies that decisionmakers should measure the effectiveness of strategic disruption operations not in the ultimate achievement of said strategic objective but instead on whether specific operations succeeded at their initial goal of delaying, degrading, or denying an adversary's ability to achieve core interests via their own preferred courses of action.

While it may seem counterintuitive to focus on the intermediate outcome of an operation, and not on its ultimate strategic effect, the need for such an approach is based upon two key aspects of our research findings. First, we found that many, if not most, strategic disruption campaigns were likely to produce indirect and delayed opportunities for strategic success over long durations, in contrast to more-direct and more-immediate campaigns that seek to disrupt the decision calculus of a competitor in a time-bound manner. Indicators of strategic success in these more-immediate campaigns are easier to measure as a result, and while quantifying the effects of military operations is obviously a desirable approach to assessing their effectiveness, it has historically led to an inefficient allocation of resources toward certain types of operations simply *because* they are measurable.[3] Measuring success against initial efforts to delay, degrade, or deny an adversary's ability to achieve their core interests through their preferred approach avoids these pitfalls by providing measurable criteria for gauging success against intermediate objectives.

Similarly, such an approach better accounts for the fact that the ultimate strategic opportunity created by a given disruption campaign may not be known at the start of the operation, or it may occur in a different domain than the initial effort to disrupt adversary-preferred strategies. Measuring the success of strategic disruption campaigns based solely on whether they are yet to achieve some ensuing strategic effect could lead to an outsized emphasis on building capabilities and conducting missions with the clearest immediate relevance to measurable military outcomes (i.e., resist, support, and target missions), and an insufficient emphasis on other capabilities and missions (i.e., influence and understand missions) that at face value are more focused on diplomatic, economic, and informational strategic outcomes that are harder to predict or measure.[4]

Strategic disruption requires deep understanding of adversary strategies and priorities. Leaders should invest in efforts to probe and understand an adversary's preferred courses of action, risk tolerance, and escalation thresholds as a foundational task. Stra-

---

[3]   This echoes the historical critique of how the U.S. military has measured its success in previous conflicts, specifically its misplaced reliance on enemy personnel losses as a measure of effectiveness in otherwise population-centric conflicts. For greater discussion, see Robinson, Egel, and Brown, 2020, p. 34; Scott Sigmund Gartner and Marissa Edson Myers, "Body Counts and 'Success' in the Vietnam and Korean Wars," *Journal of Interdisciplinary History*, Vol. 25, No. 3, 1995, pp. 377–395.

[4]   During the War on Terror, SOF similarly prioritized skill sets for direct action, often at the expense of recruitment, selection, and investments in skill sets for psychological operations, civil affairs, and UW. For discussion, see Bilms, 2021.

tegic disruption will never occur if defense policymakers and SOF planners lack an upfront understanding of an adversary's preferred courses of action to achieve core interests of their own, the adversary's alternative courses of action that may be less likely to achieve the same objectives, their risk tolerance in pursuing more-aggressive actions, and their escalation thresholds for overcoming threats to their preferred approach. A lack of understanding of an adversary's strategic design and operational priorities could not only limit SOF's ability to execute strategic disruption campaigns, it could also invite unintended escalation from ill-timed or poorly prepared actions.[5]

Overall, our analysis suggests that SOF's foundational priority in strategic disruption should be to build consistently deeper and deeper understanding of an adversary's strategic design and preferred operational approaches related to the most-relevant issues in U.S. strategic competition with that adversary. This is more than just an intelligence challenge, it points to broader implications for how SOF employ its unique pillars of capability to execute strategic disruption missions writ large and, particularly, its own capabilities for understanding through strategic reconnaissance.

Specifically, SOF should look to leverage each and every one of its ongoing operations, whether in pursuit of strategic disruption or simply in steady-state engagement with an ally or partner, to build greater understanding of how an adversary responds to the deliberate employment of SOF in ways that may affect their core interests. For example, SOF missions to support a partner along an adversary's periphery can be used to gauge that partner's responses to changes in U.S. military presence or to various operational activities conducted as part of the deployment. SOF's more-specialized capabilities for strategic reconnaissance can then focus on building deep understanding in environments where SOF operations are less likely to occur through the course of regular business working with partners. To this end, policymakers and commanders should resist the urge to refocus SOF's strategic reconnaissance capabilities solely toward more-tactical roles helping conventional forces prepare for potential wartime targets and leverage such capabilities to improve understanding of adversary-preferred strategies in competition as well.[6]

Strategic disruption requires flexible yet specific campaign plans and headquarters with a long-term focus to manage campaigns over long durations. Strategic disruption, as examined in this report, is an iterative game that involves shaping an adversary's behavior through deliberate campaigns, gauging their response, and leveraging the opportunities created by that response to achieve some broader strategic objective. As a result, SOF will require campaign plans for strategic disruption that are flexible enough to be updated often

---

[5] This is based primarily upon our finding that the real strategic benefit of efforts to frustrate adversary-preferred strategies is often in pushing an adversary toward a suboptimal approach.

[6] This risk has precedent in the Cold War, as NATO's intent for Special Forces in Europe in the 1980s transformed from preparing for resistance activities behind enemy lines toward a more tactical role as the "eyes and ears for NATO," recasting the role of SOF "from being a strategic asset to simply another surveillance system." See Cleveland and Egel, 2020, p. 19–24.

as an adversary's behavior changes over time in response to efforts to frustrate their ability to employ preferred courses of action, as new vulnerabilities emerge in their approach, or as their underlying objectives change. And yet, for policymakers to assume the risk of deliberately employing military forces for strategic disruption, such campaign plans must be discrete and specific enough to align desired disruptions to adversary-preferred strategies with a theory for how they will enable broader strategic effects.[7]

These two competing factors—flexibility and specificity—will likely require a more institutional, longer-burn approach to command and control of strategic disruption campaigns, beyond SOF's customary reliance in the War on Terror on short-term assignments of leaders and staff to temporary task forces on which the bureaucratic incentives to demonstrate success before rotating out are likely to be immense. Instead, SOF should emphasize building headquarters that are capable of taking a long view of success in strategic disruption and can retain institutional knowledge of an adversary's behavior over the course of a campaign even as operational forces are likely to rotate periodically.

Strategic disruption requires SOF to build interagency partnerships at the tactical strategic level and up through the national strategic level. In terms of how SOF should work with other instruments of power to achieve strategic disruption, our historical analysis suggests that collaboration and information-sharing with interagency partners is likely to prove essential at not just the tactical level, but also up through operational level headquarters and even at the national strategic level.

In strategic disruption, SOF are just as likely to require specific support from interagency partners at the tactical level to frustrate adversary-preferred strategies (e.g. novel sources of intelligence or technical capabilities for disruption not resident within SOF units) as they are to create opportunities that only high-level diplomacy or economic statecraft tools can successfully exploit. The more that SOF can do to create opportunities for sustained collaboration and routinized information-sharing from the bottom up and into policy discussions, the more likely they are to maximize their potential to enable multiple instruments of national power to consolidate gains following successful efforts to deny an adversary their preferred course of action.

This finding is mainly a product of the inherent uncertainty in how an adversary will respond to specific strategic disruption campaigns. Specifically, we found that not all strategic opportunities created by strategic disruption campaigns across the DIME spectrum were known in advance of the initial deliberate employment of forces, nor were they confined to the same domain as the initial effect on an adversary's strategic design. While SOF are well versed in tactical-level integration with diplomats, intelligence capabilities, development actors, and even law enforcement from decades of experience in the War on Terror, they are not as well versed in integrating with these capabilities at higher operational and stra-

---

[7] This is based on our finding that the real strategic benefit of efforts to frustrate adversary-preferred strategies is in pushing an adversary toward a suboptimal approach, and that strategic openings for other instruments of national power created by such effects often take time to materialize or occur in other domains.

tegic levels. This means that SOF in strategic competition should focus on building not just tactical-level or operational-level integration with interagency partners through structures such as interagency task forces but also flatter and more-streamlined information-sharing with senior policymakers in DoD and in other nonmilitary portions of the U.S. government.

List of Historical Strategic Disruption Campaigns

This appendix summarizes the historical case studies of strategic disruption analyzed throughout this report. This list is drawn from RAND Arroyo Center analysis of hundreds of public accounts of historical efforts by nation states and other actors to (1) use SOF or SOF-like forces to (2) execute campaigns that disrupt an adversary's preferred strategy— whether by imposing costs, creating dilemmas, or otherwise targeting vulnerabilities in that strategy—that (3) pursued or enabled friendly strategic objectives as a result.

Using these three criteria, our systematic review identified 50 publicly documented historical cases of strategic disruption campaigns, summarized in Table A.1. Though our intent was to produce as comprehensive a set of prior cases of strategic disruption as is publicly available, there are certainly examples we missed, including cases that are not in the public domain, lack a written historical record, or are simply not known to the authors despite our best efforts to document all cases.

TABLE A.1
Historical Strategic Disruption Campaigns in Chronological Order

Dates	Program (Actor)	Target	Pillar of Strategic Disruption	Intended Disruptive Effect
1920s	The Trust (USSR)	Anti-Communist monarchists ("Whites")	Influence	Undermine political-military capabilities of Russian counterrevolutionaries; deceive Western intelligence agencies about USSR's strength
1930s	Counter malign influence efforts in Latin America (FBI)	Nazi Germany	Support	Enable nations in Latin America to identify and characterize Nazi influence efforts; empower anti-Nazi influences
1940	Seizure of Fort Eben Emael (Germany)	Allies	Target	Disable defenses to allow German conventional forces to advance into Belgium
1941–1945	Kempe Tai (Japan)	Allied forces	Understand	Provide force protection of conventional forces through intelligence and counterintelligence
1941–1945	UW in Yugoslavia (SOE, OSS)	Axis Powers	Resist	Fix German and Italian conventional forces to prevent their employment in other theaters
1942	Detachment 101 (OSS)	Japan	Resist	Undermine perceptions of Japanese success in Burma using a proxy force
1944	Operation SAUERKRAUT (OSS)	Germany	Influence	Undermine morale of German forces in Italy
1944–1945	Alamo Scouts (U.S. Army)	Japan	Understand	Provide intelligence about Japanese forces to larger Allied units
1944–1945	Operation Jedburgh (OSS)	Germany	Resist	Sabotage and harass German forces in Occupied France; keep resistance leadership focused on Germany as common enemy
1948	Voice of America in Italy (U.S.)	Soviet Union	Influence	Set conditions for economic assistance and investment at the expense of Soviet influence
1949–1972	RFE/RL (CIA)	Soviet Union	Influence	Constrain Soviet power by supporting anti-communist elements in democracies at risk of takeover or weakening by the Soviet Union
1950	Trudy Jackson (USN)	North Korea	Understand	Collect intelligence in support of a conventional naval operation via clandestine insertion

Table A.1—Continued

Dates	Program (Actor)	Target	Pillar of Strategic Disruption	Intended Disruptive Effect
1950–1953	PSYOP in Korean War (U.S. Army)	North Korea	Influence	Degrade North Korea's will to fight; bolster the morale of Korean civilians
1952–1961	Project LC-CASSOCK (CIA)	East Germany	Influence	Weaken and degrade Communist sentiment in East Germany
1956–1971	Tibetan Resistance (CIA)	China	Resist	Force China to commit additional resources to Tibet to maintain control
1956–1984	Detachment A (U.S. SOF)	Soviet Union	Understand	Establish networks to sabotage civilian infrastructure in Berlin in case of a Soviet invasion of Western Europe
			Target	Target civilian infrastructure to render Berlin economically weakened in the case of a Soviet invasion
1965–1971	Prairie Fire (U.S. SOF)	Laos	Understand	Emplace sensors; conduct reconnaissance of bases and infiltration routes; direct air strikes to deny adversary safe haven
1966–present	JUSTMAGTHAI (U.S.)	Thailand	Understand	Conduct long duration mission to build Thai SOF and enable deep understanding in strategically important region
1967–1971	Salem House (U.S. SOF)	Cambodia	Understand	Collect intelligence and verification, emplace mines to deny adversary safe haven
1969	Operation Shock/Green Island Raid (Israel)	Egypt	Target	Destroy Egypt's intelligence and early-warning installations to reveal vulnerabilities and hasten conflict's conclusion
1976	Raid on Entebbe International Airport, Uganda (Israel)	PLO	Target	Demonstrate the reach of Israeli SOF and dissuade terrorist organizations from taking hostages
1979–1989	Mujahideen in Afghanistan (U.S.)	USSR	Resist	Impose costs and drain resources from the Soviet Union in the invasion of Afghanistan
1980–1992	Support to El Salvador against Communist insurgents (U.S. SOF)	USSR	Support	Prevent defeat of U.S.-friendly regime and achieve negotiated settlement to civil war

Table A.1—Continued

Dates	Program (Actor)	Target	Pillar of Strategic Disruption	Intended Disruptive Effect
1980–1992	Support to Lebanese (Iran)	Israel	Resist	Limit Israel's expansion into Lebanon and coerce Israel to withdraw its military forces from the country
1983–1987	Operation Denver (KGB, Stasi)	United States	Influence	Degrade international reputation of the United States through misinformation about origins of the HIV virus
1983–1989	QRHELPFUL (CIA)	USSR	Support	Support the development of a partner's strategic IO capability; deny adversary control over political and information environment
1987–1989	Operation Earnest Will (USN)	Kuwait-Iran	Understand	Disrupt Iranian threats to Kuwaiti oil tankers through real-time intelligence-sharing
1992	Operation Restore Hope (U.S. SOF)	Somalia	Understand	Provide force protection for civilians providing development and humanitarian assistance
1995	Operation Joint Endeavor (U.S. SOF)	Bosnia	Understand	Provide force protection for civilians providing development and humanitarian assistance
1995–1999	Joint Commission Observer (U.S. SOF)	Bosnia	Understand	Provide intelligence on local powerbrokers to enable diplomatic and military leadership
1999	Operation Matrix (U.S. SOF)	Serbia	Influence	Enforce the Dayton Accords by shaping local opinions in favor of the peace accord; establish the credibility of NATO's peacekeeping force
1999	Operation Matrix (U.S. SOF)	Serbia	Understand	Degrade support for Milošević from patronage network through detailed network mapping of malign actors to support an information campaign
1999–2007	SOF support to Plan Colombia (U.S. SOF)	FARC, Counternarcotics	Support	Set conditions for U.S. economic assistance to enable long-term development through military operations
2001	Support to Northern Alliance (U.S. SOF)	Taliban	Resist	Leverage indigenous partner forces as a primary means of overthrowing the Taliban regime in 2001

Table A.1—Continued

Dates	Program (Actor)	Target	Pillar of Strategic Disruption	Intended Disruptive Effect
2001–2014	Operation Enduring Freedom—Philippines (U.S. SOF)	VEO	Support	Reduce transnational terrorist threat and support for threat groups in the Philippines; professionalize and develop partner forces; enhance bilateral relationship
2003	Kurdish Peshmerga forces (U.S. SOF)	Iraq	Resist	Leverage indigenous partner forces as a shaping effort in support of larger, conventional force operations
2003–present	Build Iraq's CTS counterterrorism capability (U.S. SOF)	VEO	Support	Enable CTS to maintain internal stability in Iraq; promote multiethnic Iraqi security institutions as a counterweight to sectarian influences
2007	Destruction of Al Kibar nuclear reactor (Israel)	Syria	Target	Set back Syria's nuclear program; signal resolve and capability to nuclear proliferators in region
2008	Operation Jacque (U.S. SOF)	FARC	Understand	U.S.-enabled Colombian operation to free an imprisoned journalist; deny FARC efforts to raise revenue; and impose costs
2010	Sabotage of Iranian nuclear program (unknown)	Iran	Target	Set back Iran's nuclear program
2011	Bin Laden raid (U.S.)	Al-Qaeda	Target	Degrade adversary command and control; erode ideological appeal
2011–2017	Observant Compass (U.S. SOF)	LRA	Influence	Induce fighters to defect from the LRA

Table A.1—Continued

Dates	Program (Actor)	Target	Pillar of Strategic Disruption	Intended Disruptive Effect
2013–2014	Propaganda campaign in Eastern Ukraine (Russia)	Ukraine	Resist	Destabilize eastern Ukraine through propaganda and UW to prevent Kyiv from asserting authority over breakaway regions
2014	Bosnian flood response (U.S. SOF)	Serbia, Russia	Understand	Leverage deep understanding of civil actors to promote legitimacy of Bosnian armed forces as a counterweight to Serbian and Russian influence
2014–2022	Security sector reform in Ukraine (U.S.)	Russia	Support	Counter Russian efforts to degrade Ukrainian government and military effectiveness through malign influence and corruption
2014–present	Build Baltic total defense capacity (U.S.)	Russia	Resist	Build NATO and Baltic states' capacity for total defense in the event of a Russian occupation
2014–present	Fentanyl crisis (China)	United States	Resist	Precipitate a drain on the U.S. economy and U.S. society by neglecting to constrain the proliferation of fentanyl precursors entering the United States via cartels
2015	Abu Sayyaf raid (U.S.)	ISIS	Target	Collect key intelligence to enable more-effective targeting by conventional forces
2015 – 2019	Support to pro-regime forces in Syria (Russia)	Anti-Assad forces	Support	Deny anti-Assad forces a military victory, maintain access and influence for power projection
2020	COVID-19 propaganda (China)	United States	Influence	Degrade international reputation of the United States through misinformation about origins of the COVID-19 pandemic and U.S. pandemic response
2021	Colonial Pipeline ransomware attack (Russia)	United States	Target	Disrupt U.S. oil and gas distribution at the national level

Abbreviations

CCP	Chinese Communist Party
CIA	Central Intelligence Agency
COVID-19	coronavirus disease 2019
CTS	counterterrorism service
DIME	diplomatic, informational, military, and economic
DIMEFIL	diplomatic, informational, economic, financial, intelligence, and law enforcement
DoD	U.S. Department of Defense
EMSO	electromagnetic spectrum operations
FARC	Revolutionary Armed Forces of Colombia
FBI	Federal Bureau of Investigation
HIV	human immunodeficiency virus
IO	information operations
JUSTMAGTHAI	Joint United States Military Advisory Group Thailand
KGB	Committee for State Security of the Soviet Union
LRA	Lord's Resistance Army
MIDFIELD	military, informational, diplomatic, financial, intelligence, economic, law, and development
NATO	North Atlantic Treaty Organization
NDS	National Defense Strategy
OSS	Office of Strategic Services
PLO	Palestine Liberation Organization
PRC	People's Republic of China
PSYOP	psychological operation
RFE/RL	Radio Free Europe, Radio Liberation
SOE	Special Operations Executive
SOF	special operations forces
USASOC	United States Army Special Operations Command
USN	United States Navy
USSOCOM	United States Special Operations Command
USSR	Union of Soviet Socialist Republics
UW	unconventional warfare
VEO	violent extremist organization
VOA	Voice of America

References

Abuza, Zachary, "America Should Be Realistic About its Alliance with Thailand," *War on the Rocks*, January 2, 2020.

Aragon, Bethany C., "Employing Information as an Instrument of National Power," U.S. Army War College, 2016.

Arkin, William, and Robert Windrem, "The Other Kosovo War," MSNBC, August 29, 2001.

Army Doctrine Publication 3-05, *Army Special Operations*, U.S. Department of the Army, July 2019.

Atlamazoglou, Stavros, "The U.S. Is Scrambling to Deal with Cyberattacks, and That May Mean New Roles and Missions for Special-Ops Units," *Business Insider*, June 10, 2021.

Azizian, Nazanin, *Easier to Get into War Than to Get Out: The Case of Afghanistan*, Harvard University Belfer Center, August 2021.

Becker, David W., "Coming in from the Cold . . . War: Defense Humint Services Support to Military Operations Other Than War," U.S. Army Command and General Staff College, 2000.

Bilms, Kevin, "Past as Prelude? Envisioning the Future of Special Operations," The Strategy Bridge, November 12, 2021.

Blanchard, Jean-Marc F., Edward D. Mansfield, and Norrin M. Ripsman, "The Political Economy of National Security: Economic Statecraft, Interdependence, and International Conflict," *Security Studies*, Vol. 9, Nos. 1–2, 2007.

Blanchard, Jean-Marc F., Edward D. Mansfield, and Norrin M. Ripsman, eds., *Power and the Purse: Economic Statecraft, Interdependence and National Security*, Routledge, December 2013.

Brands, Hal, "The Dark Art of Political Warfare: A Primer," American Enterprise Institute, February 2020.

Brands, Hal, and Tim Nichols, *Cost Imposition in the Contact Layer: Special Operations Forces and Great-Power Rivalry*, American Enterprise Institute, July 2021.

Brangetto, Pascal, and Matthijs A. Veenendaal, "Influence Cyber Operations: The Use of Cyberattacks in Support of Influence Operations," paper presented at the 8th International Conference on Cyber Conflict, 2016.

Bredenkamp, Nicholas A., and Mark Grzegorzewski, "Supporting Resistance Movements in Cyberspace," *Special Operations Journal*, Vol. 7, No. 1, April 2021.

Brown, Ethan, "After Afghanistan, U.S. Forces Are Ill-Prepared for Electronic Warfare Elsewhere," *The Hill*, December 7, 2021.

Broyles, David A., and Brody Blankenship, *The Role of Special Operations Forces in Global Competition*, Center for Naval Analyses, April 2017.

Carson, Austin, and Keren Yarhi-Milo, "Covert Communication: The Intelligibility and Credibility of Signaling in Secret," *Security Studies*, Vol. 26, No. 1, 2016.

Carter, Daniel, "Detachment A Recognized for Cold War Efforts in Commemorative Stone Laying Ceremony," United States Army Special Operations Command News Service, January 31, 2014.

CIA—*See* U.S. Central Intelligence Agency.

Cleveland, Charles T., "Command and Control of the Joint Commission Observer Program: U.S. Army Special Forces in Bosnia," United States Army War College, 2001.

Cleveland, Charles T., and Daniel Egel, *The American Way of Irregular War: An Analytical Memoir,* RAND Corporation, PE-A301-1, 2020. As of July 18, 2022: https://www.rand.org/pubs/perspectives/PEA301-1.html

Cleveland, Charles T., James B. Linder, and Ronald Dempsey, "Special Operations Doctrine: Is It Needed?" *PRISM*, Vol. 6, No. 3, December 2016.

Cohen, Raphael S., "It's Time to Drop 'Competition' in the National Defense Strategy," *The Hill*, May 18, 2021.

Collins, Elizabeth M., "First to Go: Green Berets Remember Earliest Mission in Afghanistan," U.S. Army Public Affairs, February 8, 2017.

Crist, David B., "Joint Special Operations in Support of Earnest Will," *Joint Forces Quarterly*, Autumn/Winter 2001–2002.

De Wit, Daniel, "Fake News for the Resistance: The OSS and the Nexus of Psychological Warfare and Resistance Operations in World War II," *Journal of Advanced Military Studies*, Vol. 12, No. 1, Spring 2021.

Department of Defense Directive 3000.07, *Irregular Warfare*, U.S. Department of Defense, May 12, 2017.

DoD—*See* U.S. Department of Defense.

Dudley, Sara, Kevin D. Stringer, and Steve Ferenzi, "Beyond Direct Action: A Counter-Threat Finance Approach to Competition," Kingston Consortium on International Security, 2021.

Duggan, Patrick Michael, "Strategic Development of Special Warfare in Cyberspace," *Joint Forces Quarterly*, No. 79, October 1, 2015.

Duke, J. Darren, Rex L. Phillips, and Christopher J. Conover, "Challenges in Coalition Unconventional Warfare: The Allied Campaign in Yugoslavia, 1941–1945," *Joint Forces Quarterly*, No. 75, September 30, 2014.

Dunham, Mikel, *Buddha's Warriors: The Story of the CIA-Backed Tibetan Freedom Fighters, the Chinese Communist Invasion, and the Ultimate Fall of Tibet*, Penguin, 2004.

Ebitz, Amy, *The Use of Military Diplomacy in Great Power Competition: Lessons Learned from the Marshall Plan*, Brookings Institution, February 12, 2019.

Ehrensvärd Jensen, Lars H., "Special Operations: Myths and Facts," Royal Danish Defence College, 2014.

Ekman, Kenneth P., *Winning the Peace Through Cost Imposition*, Brookings Institution, May 2014.

Faint, Charles, and Michael Harris, "F3EAD: Ops/Intel Fusion 'Feeds' the SOF Targeting Process," *Small Wars Journal*, January 31, 2012.

Fane, Daria, "After Afghanistan: The Decline of Soviet Military Prestige," *Washington Quarterly*, Vol. 13, No. 2, Spring 1990.

Felbab-Brown, Vanda, "The Implications of Osama bin Laden's Death for the War in Afghanistan and Global Counterterrorism Efforts," Brookings Institution, May 2, 2011.

Fiala, Otto C., Kirk Smith, and Anders Löfberg, "Resistance Operating Concept (ROC)" Joint Special Operations University Press, 2020.

Field Manual 3-05.6, *Army Special Operations Forces Aviation Operations*, U.S. Department of the Army, October 2000.

Field Manual 3-05.130, *Army Special Operations Forces Unconventional Warfare*, U.S. Department of the Army, September 2008.

Field Manual 3-12, *Cyberspace and Electronic Warfare Operations*, U.S. Department of the Army, August 2021.

Finel, Bernard I., "Much Ado About Competition: The Logic and Utility of Competitive Strategy," West Point Modern War Institute, February 1, 2022.

Flanagan, Stephen J., Jan Osburg, Anika Binnendijk, Marta Kepe, and Andrew Radin, *Deterring Russian Aggression in the Baltic States Through Resilience and Resistance*, RAND Corporation, RR-2779-OSD, 2019. As of July 18, 2022: https://www.rand.org/pubs/research_reports/RR2779.html

Friend, Alice Hunt, and Shannon Culbertson, "Special Obfuscations: The Strategic Uses of Special Operations Forces," Center for Strategic and International Studies, March 6, 2020.

Galeotti, Mark, "The Three Faces of Russian Spetsnaz in Syria," *War on the Rocks*, March 21, 2016.

Garamone, Jim, "Concept of Integrated Deterrence Will Be Key to National Defense Strategy, DOD Official Says," *Department of Defense News*, December 8, 2021.

Gartner, Scott Sigmund, and Marissa Edson Myers, "Body Counts and 'Success' in the Vietnam and Korean Wars," *Journal of Interdisciplinary History*, Vol. 25, No. 3, 1995.

Gheciu, Alexandra, "Security Institutions as Agents of Socialization? NATO and the 'New Europe,'" *International Organization*, Vol. 59, No. 4, Fall 2005.

Gladding, Ryan S., and Sean P. McQuade, "Cyber-Enabled Unconventional Warfare: The Convergence of Cyberspace, Social Mobilization, and Special Warfare," Naval Postgraduate School, December 2015.

Goldstein, Frank L., and Benjamin F. Findley, eds., *Psychological Operations: Principles and Case Studies*, Air University Press, 1996.

Greenberg, Andy, "The Untold Story of NotPetya, the Most Devastating Cyberattack in History," WIRED, August 22, 2018.

Haddick, Robert, *How Do SOF Contribute to Comprehensive Deterrence?* Joint Special Operations University Report 17-11, 2017.

Heath, Timothy R., Derek Grossman, and Asha Clark, *China's Quest for Global Primacy*, RAND Corporation, RR-A447-1, 2021. As of June 10, 2022: https://www.rand.org/pubs/research_reports/RRA447-1.html

Heath, Timothy R., Eric Robinson, Christian Curriden, Derek Grossman, Sale Lilly, Daniel Egel, and Gabrielle Tarini, *Disrupting the Chinese Military in Competition and Low-Intensity Conflict: An Analysis of People's Liberation Army Missions, Tasks, and Potential Vulnerabilities*, RAND Corporation, 2023.

Hoevelmann, Kaitlyn, "The Economic Costs of the Opioid Epidemic," Federal Reserve Bank of St. Louis, September 4, 2019.

Irwin, Will, and Isaiah Wilson III, *The Fourth Age of SOF: The Use and Utility of Special Operations Forces in a New Age*, Joint Special Operations University Report 22-1, 2022.

Jennings, Ralph, "Changing of the Guard: Civilian Protection for an Evolving Military," *PRISM*, Vol. 4, No. 2, December 2013.

Jennings, Ralph, "Why the Philippines Picked America over China," *Voice of America*, August 5, 2021.

Johnson, A. Ross, "Managing Media Influence Operations: Lessons from Radio Free Europe/ Radio Liberty," *International Journal of Intelligence and Counterintelligence*, Vol. 31, No. 4, December 20, 2018.

Joint Doctrine Note 1-18, *Strategy*, U.S. Department of Defense Joint Chiefs of Staff, April 25, 2018.

Joint Publication 1-0, *Doctrine for the Armed Forces of the United States*, U.S. Department of Defense, July 12, 2017.

Joint Publication 3-05, *Special Operations*, U.S. Department of Defense, July 16, 2014.

Joint Publication 3-12, *Cyberspace Operations*, U.S. Department of Defense, June 8, 2018.

Joint Publication 3-13, *Information Operations*, U.S. Department of Defense, November 20, 2014.

Joint Publication 3-13.4, *Military Deception*, U.S. Department of Defense, January 26, 2012.

Joint Publication 3-22, *Foreign Internal Defense*, U.S. Department of Defense, February 2, 2021.

Jones, Seth G., *A Covert Action: Reagan, the CIA, and the Cold War Struggle in Poland*, W. W. Norton, 2018a.

Jones, Seth G., "Going on the Offensive: A U.S. Strategy to Combat Russian Information Warfare," Center for Strategic and International Studies, October 2018b.

Jones, Seth G., *Three Dangerous Men: Russia, China, Iran, and the Rise of Irregular Warfare*, W. W. Norton, 2021a.

Jones, Seth G., "The Future of Competition: U.S. Adversaries and the Growth of Irregular Warfare," Center for Strategic and International Studies, February 4, 2021b.

Jordan, Jenna, "Attacking the Leader, Missing the Mark: Why Terrorist Groups Survive Decapitation Strikes," *International Security*, Vol. 34, No. 4, 2014.

Kashkett, Steven, "Special Operations and Diplomacy: A Unique Nexus," American Foreign Service Association, June 2017.

Kassel, Whitney, and Philip Reiner, "'Cyber FID': The Role of Cyber in Foreign Internal Defense," in Zachary S. Davis, Frank Gac, Christopher Rager, Philip Reiner, and Jennifer Snow, eds., *Strategic Latency Unleashed: The Role of Technology in a Revisionist Global Order and the Implications for Special Operations Forces*, Lawrence Livermore National Laboratory, 2021.

Khalidi, Ahmed S., "The War of Attrition," *Journal of Palestine Studies*, Vol. 3, No. 1, 1973.

Kidwell, Deborah, "Operation RESTORE HOPE (The OSI in Somalia)," U.S. Air Force Office of Special Investigations, July 9, 2020.

Kilcullen, David, "The Evolution of Unconventional Warfare," *Scandinavian Journal of Military Studies*, 2019.

Kiras, James, "Special Operations and Strategies of Attrition," *Military Strategy Magazine*, Vol. 2, No. 4, 2012.

Knights, Michael, and Alex Mello, "The Best Thing America Built in Iraq: Iraq's Counter-Terrorism Service and the Long War Against Militancy," *War on the Rocks*, July 19, 2017.

Kramer, Mark, "Lessons from Operation 'Denver,' the KGB's Massive AIDS Disinformation Campaign," MIT Press Reader, May 26, 2020.

L., Andrew, Mick Mulroy, and Ken Tovo, "Irregular Warfare: A Case Study in CIA and U.S. Army Special Forces Operations in Northern Iraq, 2002–3," Middle East Institute, August 2021.

Ladwig, Walter C., "Influencing Clients in Counterinsurgency: U.S. Involvement in El Salvador's Civil War, 1979–92," *International Security*, Vol. 41, No. 1, Summer 2016.

Lanning, Michael J., and Edward G. Michaels, "A Business Is a Value Delivery System," McKinsey Staff Paper No. 41, June 1988.

Larson, Eric V., Richard E. Darilek, Daniel Gibran, Brian Nichiporuk, Amy Richardson, Lowell H. Schwartz, and Cathryn Quantic Thurston, *Foundations of Effective Influence Operations: A Framework for Enhancing Army Capabilities*, RAND Corporation, MG-654-A, 2009. As of July 18, 2022:
https://www.rand.org/pubs/monographs/MG654.html

Lee, Doowan, "Cost Imposition: The Key to Making Great Power Competition an Actionable Strategy," West Point Modern War Institute, April 8, 2021.

Lendvay, Ronald L., "Shadows of Stuxnet: Recommendations for U.S. Policy on Critical Infrastructure Cyber Defense Derived from the Stuxnet Attack," Naval Postgraduate School, March 2016.

Lewis, Larry, and Sarah Holewinski, "Changing of the Guard: Civilian Protection for an Evolving Military," *PRISM*, Vol. 4, No. 2, December 2013.

Little, Ralph, and Paul Pilliod, "Drug Warfare: The Confluence of Jihadist and China," North Florida High Intensity Drug Trafficking Areas Assessment 2017-1, August 2017.

Long, Austin, Todd C. Helmus, S. Rebecca Zimmerman, Christopher M. Schnaubelt, and Peter Chalk, *Building Special Operations Partnerships in Afghanistan and Beyond: Challenges and Best Practices from Afghanistan, Iraq, and Colombia*, RAND Corporation, RR-713-OSD, 2015. As of May 26, 2023:
https://www.rand.org/pubs/research_reports/RR713.html

Long, Austin, "The Limits of Special Operations Forces," *PRISM*, Vol. 6, No. 3, 2016.

Lopez, Todd C., "Parent Services Integration a Top Priority for Special Operations Components," Department of Defense News, May 2, 2022.

Lumbaca, J. "Lumpy," "The U.S.-Thailand ARSOF Relationship," *Special Warfare*, 2012.

Lyall, Jason, and Isaiah Wilson III, "Rage Against the Machines: Explaining Outcomes in Counterinsurgency Wars," *International Organization*, Vol. 63, No. 1, Winter 2009.

Machain, Carla Martinez, "Exporting Influence: U.S. Military Training as Soft Power," *Journal of Conflict Resolution*, Vol. 65, Nos. 2–3, 2020.

MacLachlan, Karolina, "Corruption as Statecraft: Using Corrupt Practices as Foreign Policy Tools," Transparency International: Defense and Security, November 18, 2019.

Madden, Dan, Dick Hoffmann, Michael Johnson, Fred T. Krawchuk, Bruce R. Nardulli, John E. Peters, Linda Robinson, and Abby Doll, *Toward Operational Art in Special Warfare*, RAND Corporation, RR-779-A, 2016. As of July 18, 2022:
https://www.rand.org/pubs/research_reports/RR779.html

Maier, Christopher P., "Statement for the Record," opening statement, Committee on Armed Services, United States Senate hearing, April 5, 2022.

Makovsky, David, "The Silent Strike: How Israel Bombed a Syrian Nuclear Installation and Kept it Secret," *New Yorker*, September 10, 2012.

Marvin, Andrew R., "Operation Earnest Will: The U.S. Foreign Policy Behind U.S. Naval Operations in the Persian Gulf 1987–89; A Curious Case," *Naval War College Review*, 2020.

Mazarr, Michael J., *Understanding Deterrence*, RAND Corporation, PE-295-RC, 2018. As of July 18, 2022:
https://www.rand.org/pubs/perspectives/PE295.html

McRaven, William H., "The Theory of Special Operations," Naval Postgraduate School, June 1993.

McRaven, William H., *Spec Ops: Case Studies in Operational Warfare: Theory and Practice*, Presidio Press, 1996.

Messenger, David A., "'Against the Grain': Special Operations Executive in Spain, 1941–45," *Intelligence and National Security*, Vol. 20, No. 1, 2000.

Miller, James E., "Taking Off the Gloves: The United States and the Italian Elections of 1948," *Diplomatic History*, Vol. 7, No. 1, 1983.

Mitchell, Mark, "Strategic Leverage: Information Operations and Special Operations Forces," Naval Postgraduate School, 1999.

Mitre, Jim, and Andre Gellerman, *Defining DoD's Role in Gray Zone Competition*, Center for a New American Security, August 24, 2020.

Moran, Michael, "Psyops Employed to Sap Iraqi Spirit," *NBC News*, December 2003.

Morris, Lyle J., Michael J. Mazarr, Jeffrey W. Hornung, Stephanie Pezard, Anika Binnendijk, and Marta Kepe, *Gaining Competitive Advantage in the Gray Zone: Response Options for Coercive Aggression Below the Threshold of Major War*, RAND Corporation, RR-2942-OSD, 2019. As of July 18, 2022:
https://www.rand.org/pubs/research_reports/RR2942.html

Oliker, Olga, Lynn E. Davis, Keith Crane, Andrew Radin, Celeste Ward Gventer, Susanne Sondergaard, James T. Quinlivan, Stephan B. Seabrook, Jacopo Bellasio, Bryan Frederick, Andriy Bega, and Jakub Hlavka, *Security Sector Reform in Ukraine*, RAND Corporation, RR-1475-1-UIA, 2016. As of July 18, 2022:
https://www.rand.org/pubs/research_reports/RR1475-1.html

Ottis, Rain, "Analysis of the 2007 Cyber Attacks Against Estonia from the Information Warfare Perspective," proceedings of the 7th European Conference on Information Warfare and Security, Cooperative Cyber Defence Centre of Excellence, 2008.

Paddock, Alfred H., Jr., "Military Psychological Operations," in Carnes Lord and Frank R. Barnett, eds., *Political Warfare and Psychological Operations: Rethinking the U.S. Approach*, National Defense University Press, 1989.

Pascoli, Sean W., and Mark Grzegorzewski, "Technology Adoption in Unconventional Warfare," *The Cyber Defense Review*, 2021.

Peck, Michael, "This Special Forces Unit Was Trained to Attack Russia from Germany During the Cold War," *The National Interest,* July 2020.

Pelleriti, John A., Michael Maloney, David C. Cox, Heather J. Sullivan, J. Eric Piskura, and Montigo J. Hawkins, "The Insufficiency of U.S. Irregular Warfare Doctrine," *Joint Forces Quarterly*, No. 93, 2nd Quarter 2019.

Petit, Brian S., *Breaking Through the Tension: The Operational Art of Special Operations in Phase Zero*, School of Advanced Military Studies, United States Army Command and General Staff College, 2013.

Pomerlau, Mark, "Army Special Forces Want to Integrate More with Other Military Units on Info Warfare," C4ISRNet, August 19, 2021.

Porche, Isaac R., III, Christopher Paul, Chad C. Serena, Colin P. Clarke, Erin-Elizabeth Johnson, and Drew Herrick, *Tactical Cyber: Building a Strategy for Cyber Support to Corps and Below*, RAND Corporation, RR-1600-A, 2017. As of May 3, 2023:
https://www.rand.org/pubs/research_reports/RR1600.html

Porche, Isaac R., III, Christopher Paul, Michael York, Chad C. Serena, Jerry M. Sollinger, Elliot Axelband, Endy Y. Min, and Bruce J. Held, *Redefining Information Warfare Boundaries for an Army in a Wireless World*, RAND Corporation, MG-1113-A, 2013. As of May 3, 2023:
https://www.rand.org/pubs/monographs/MG1113.html

Radin, Andrew, "Chapter 6: Defense Reform in Ukraine," *Institution Building in Weak States*, Georgetown University Press, 2020.

Randolph, R. Sean, *The United States and Thailand: Allied Dynamics, 1950–1985*, Institute of East Asian Studies, University of California, Berkeley, 1986.

Rid, Thomas, *Active Measures: The Secret History of Disinformation and Political Warfare*, Farrar, Straus, and Giroux, 2020.

Roach, James S., "Joint Special Operations Targeting: An Alternate Scheme," U.S. Army War College, 1989.

Robinson, Eric, "The Missing, Irregular Half of Great Power Competition," West Point Modern War Institute, September 8, 2020.

Robinson, Linda, "The Future of Special Operations: Beyond Kill and Capture," *Foreign Affairs*, November/December 2012.

Robinson, Linda, "The SOF Experience in the Philippines and the Implications for Future Defense Strategy," *PRISM*, Vol. 6 No. 3, December 7, 2016.

Robinson, Linda, Daniel Egel, and Ryan Andrew Brown, *Measuring the Effectiveness of Special Operations*, RAND Corporation, RR-2504-A, 2019. As of July 18, 2022:
https://www.rand.org/pubs/research_reports/RR2504.html

Robinson, Linda, Todd C. Helmus, Raphael S. Cohen, Alireza Nader, Andrew Radin, Madeline Magnuson, and Katya Migacheva, *Modern Political Warfare: Current Practices and Possible Responses*, RAND Corporation, RR-1772-A, 2018. As of July 18, 2022:
https://www.rand.org/pubs/research_reports/RR1772.html

Rosenau, William, *Special Operations Forces and Elusive Enemy Ground Targets*, RAND Corporation, MR-1408-AF, 2001. As of July 18, 2022:
https://www.rand.org/pubs/monograph_reports/MR1408.html

Ruffo, Val L., "The Application of Counterintelligence Force Protection Source Operations (CFSO) in the U.S. Pacific Command," U.S. Army Command and General Staff College, 1996.

Ryan, Kristen, ed., *Resistance and the Cyber Domain*, United States Army Special Operations Command and Johns Hopkins University Applied Physics Laboratory, 2019.

Schaner, Eric X., "What Is Military Information Power?" *Marine Corps Gazette*, April 2020.

Schechner, Sam, "Ukraine's 'IT Army' Has Hundreds of Thousands of Hackers, Kyiv Says," *Wall Street Journal*, March 4, 2022.

Schoen, Fletcher, and Christopher J. Lamb, "Deception, Disinformation, and Strategic Communications: How One Interagency Group Made a Major Difference," National Defense University Institute for National Strategic Studies, *Strategic Perspectives*, No. 11, June 2012.

Sinai, Tamir, "Eyes on Target: 'Stay-Behind' Forces During the Cold War," *War in History*, Vol. 28, No. 3, 2021.

Smeets, Max, and Brita Achberger, "Cyber Hacktivists Are Busy Undermining Putin's Invasion," *Washington Post*, May 13, 2022.

Spulak, Robert G., Jr., *A Theory of Special Operations*, Joint Special Operations University Report 07-7, October 2007.

Stejskal, James, *Special Forces Berlin: Clandestine Cold War Operations of the US Army's Elite, 1956–1990*, Casemate, 2017.

Szubin, Adam, "Remarks of Acting Under Secretary Adam Szubin on Countering the Financing of Terrorism at the Paul H. Nitze School of Advanced International Studies," press release, U.S. Department of the Treasury, October 10, 2016.

Taft, John, Liz Gormisky, and Joe Mariani, "Special Operations Forces and Great Power Competition: Talent, Technology, and Organizational Change in the New Threat Environment," Deloitte Insights, 2019.

Taylor, Curt, and Larry Kay, "Putting the Enemy Between a Rock and a Hard Place: Multi-Domain Operations in Practice," West Point Modern War Institute, August 27, 2019.

Terrill, W. Andrew, "The Nature and Value of Commando Operations During the Egyptian Israeli War of Attrition," *Small Wars and Insurgencies*, Vol. 8, No. 2, 1997.

Tolbert, Julian, "Crony Attack: Strategic Attack's Silver Bullet?" School of Advanced Air and Space Studies, November 2006.

Tompkins, Paul, Joe Tonon, Erin Hahn, and Guillermo Puncczuk, "Unconventional Warfare Study Research and Writing Guide," U.S. Army Special Operations Command and the Johns Hopkins University Applied Physics Laboratory, undated.

Tracey, Jared M., "A Team Approach: PSYOP and LRA Defection in 2012," *Veritas Journal of Army Special Operations History*, Vol. 15, No. 1, 2019.

Tsvetanov, Tsvetan, and Srishti Slaria, "The Effect of the Colonial Pipeline Shutdown on Gasoline Prices," *Economics Letters*, No. 209, December 2021.

Tucker, Patrick, "Army SOF Units Are Getting Smaller, More Self-Reliant as Focus Shifts to China, Russia," *Defense One*, May 20, 2021.

U.S. Army Futures Command, "Army Futures Command Concept for Special Operations 2028," September 18, 2020.

U.S. Army Special Operations Command, *Little Green Men: A Primer on Modern Russian Unconventional Warfare, Ukraine 2013–2014*, United States Army Special Operations Command and Johns Hopkins University Applied Physics Lab, undated.

U.S. Army Special Operations Command, "Unconventional Warfare Pocket Guide," April 5, 2016.

U.S. Army Special Operations Command, "Communicating the ARSOF Narrative and Setting the Course to 2035," John F. Kennedy Special Warfare Center and School, 2017.

U.S. Army Training and Doctrine Command Pamphlet 525-3-1, *The U.S. Army Operating Concept: Win in a Complex World*, October 7, 2014.

U.S. Army Training and Doctrine Command Pamphlet 525-3-1, *The U.S in Multi-Domain Operations, 2028,* U.S. Department of the Army, December 6, 2018.

U.S. Central Intelligence Agency, "The 'Glorious Amateurs' of OSS: A Sisterhood of Spies," webpage, April 6, 2022. As of July 18, 2022:
https://www.cia.gov/stories/story/glorious-amateurs-of-oss-sisterhood-of-spies/

U.S. Commission on Combating Synthetic Opioid Trafficking, *Final Report,* February 2022.

U.S. Department of Defense, *Summary of the Department of Defense Cyber Strategy,* 2018a.

U.S. Department of Defense, *Summary of the 2018 National Defense Strategy,* January 2018b.

U.S. Department of Defense, *Summary of the Irregular Warfare Annex to the National Defense Strategy,* 2020a.

U.S. Department of Defense, *Electromagnetic Spectrum Superiority Strategy,* October 2020b.

U.S. Department of Defense, *DoD Dictionary of Military and Associated Terms,* November 2021.

U.S. Department of Defense, *Fact Sheet: 2022 National Defense Strategy,* fact sheet, March 2022.

U.S. Department of State, "Global Engagement Center (R/GEC)," undated.

U.S. Department of State, "33.7 Memorandum for the Special Group," in *Foreign Relations of the United States, 1964-1968*: Vol. XXX, *China,* January 9, 1964.

U.S. Department of the Air Force, "Special Reconnaissance," webpage, undated.

U.S. Department of the Army, *The Army in Military Competition,* Chief of Staff Paper, No. 2, March 1, 2021.

U.S. Drug Enforcement Administration, *Fentanyl Flow to the United States,* Intelligence Report DEA-DCT-DIR-008-20, January 2020.

U.S. Global Leadership Coalition, "Plan Colombia: A Development Success Story," 2017.

U.S. Senate Armed Services Committee, "Bombings in Cambodia," in *Hearings, Ninety-Third Congress, First Session,* U.S. Government Publishing Office, 1973.

U.S. Senate Armed Services Committee, "Part 5: Emerging Threats and Capabilities," in *Senate Hearing 113-465, Part 5,* U.S. Government Publishing Office, 2014.

U.S. Senate Armed Services Committee, "To Receive Testimony on United States Special Operations Command and United States Cyber Command in Review of the Defense Authorization Request for Fiscal Year 2022 and the Future Years Defense Program," hearing transcript, March 25, 2021.

Valeriano, Brandon, "Cost Imposition Is the Point: Understanding U.S. Cyber Operations and the Strategy Behind Achieving Effects," Lawfare, March 27, 2020.

van Hooren, Jonas, "The Imperative Symbiotic Relationship Between SOF and Cyber: How Dutch Special Operation Forces Can Support Cyber Operations," Naval Postgraduate School, 2019.

Votel, Joseph L., Charles T. Cleveland, Charles T. Connett, and Will Irwin, "Unconventional Warfare in the Gray Zone, " *Joint Forces Quarterly,* Vol. 80, No. 1, January 2016.

Wasser, Becca, and Stacie L. Pettyjohn, "Why the Pentagon Should Abandon 'Strategic Competition,'" *Foreign Policy,* October 19, 2021.

Wasser, Becca, Stacie L. Pettyjohn, Jeffrey Martini, Alexandra T. Evans, Karl P. Mueller, Nathaniel Edenfield, Gabrielle Tarini, Ryan Haberman, and Jalen Zeman, *The Air War Against the Islamic State: The Role of Airpower in Operation Inherent Resolve*, RAND Corporation, RR-A388-1, 2021. As of July 18, 2022:
https://www.rand.org/pubs/research_reports/RRA388-1.html

Watts, Stephen, Alexander Noyes, and Gabrielle Tarini, *Competition and Governance in African Security Sectors: Integrating U.S. Strategic Objectives*, RAND Corporation, RR-A567-1, 2022. As of July 18, 2022:
https://www.rand.org/pubs/research_reports/RRA567-1.html.

Watts, Stephen, Sean M. Zeigler, Kimberly Jackson, Caitlin McCulloch, Joe Cheravitch, Marta Kepe, *Countering Russia: The Role of Special Operations Forces in Strategic Competition*, RAND Corporation, RR-A412-1, 2021. As of July 18, 2022:
https://www.rand.org/pubs/research_reports/RRA412-1.html

Westberg, Anders, "In Silence Toward the Unknown: Principles of Special Reconnaissance and Surveillance," Naval Postgraduate School, 2016. White House, *Interim National Security Strategic Guidance*, March 2021.

Williams, Lauren C., "Cyber Assistance Ranks High on National Guard Requested Services, Chief Says," *FCW*, May 10, 2022.

Winkie, Davis, "Less Door-Kicking, More Resistance: Inside Army SOF's Return to Unconventional Warfare," *Army Times*, September 9, 2021.

Wittmer, Luke A., "Covert Coercion: A Formal Analysis of Unconventional Warfare as an Interstate Coercive Policy Option," Naval Postgraduate School, June 2013.

Wolf, Charles, Jr., K. C. Yeh, Edmund Brunner, Jr., Aaron Gurwitz, Marilee Lawrence, *The Costs of the Soviet Empire*, RAND Corporation, R-3073/1-NA, 1984. As of July 18, 2022:
https://www.rand.org/pubs/reports/R3073z1.html